They Shoot Writers, Don't They?

**Metropolitan College of NY
Library - 7th Floor
60 West Street
New York, NY 10006**

They Shoot Writers, Don't They?

Edited by George Theiner

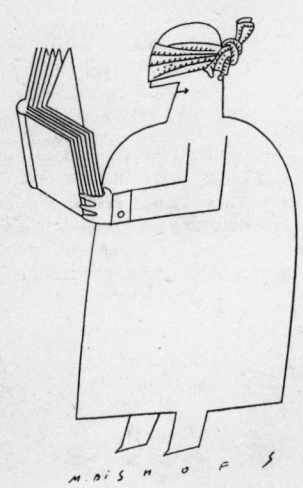

faber and faber
LONDON · BOSTON

This collection first published in 1984
by Faber and Faber Limited
3 Queen Square London WC1N 3AU
Printed in Great Britain by
Whitstable Litho Ltd., Whitstable, Kent
All rights reserved

This collection © Writers and Scholars International Ltd.,
publishers of *Index on Censorship*, 1984
Illustrations © Maris Bishofs, 1984

CONDITIONS OF SALE
*This book is sold subject to the condition that it shall not,
by way of trade or otherwise, be lent, resold, hired out or otherwise
circulated without the publisher's prior consent in any form of binding
or cover other than that in which it is published and without a similar
condition including this condition being imposed on the subsequent
purchaser*

British Library Cataloguing in Publication Data

They shoot writers, don't they?
1. Censorship
I. Theiner, George
363.3'1   PN156

ISBN 0–571–13260–X

Contents

Acknowledgements	page 9
Introduction	11
GEORGE THEINER	
Note	17
STEPHEN SPENDER	
How *Index on Censorship* Started	19
MICHAEL SCAMMELL	
God Keep Me from Going Mad	29
ALEXANDER SOLZHENITSYN	
Letter to Europeans	32
GEORGE MANGAKIS	
All You Need is a Typewriter	43
JAN VLADISLAV	
Variation on a Theme	52
IVAN KLÍMA	
Open Letter to President Husák	57
TOM STOPPARD	
Free Thoughts on Toilet Paper	60
NGŨGĨ WA THIONG'O	
Camara Laye—Involuntary Exile	66
DENIS HERBSTEIN	
Searching for the Truth	74
WEI JINGSHENG	
Casualties of Censorship	84
SALMAN RUSHDIE	
Manuscripts Banned and Destroyed	88
PRAMOEDYA ANANTA TOER	
From the Darkness	95
KIM CHI-HA	

Contents

My Ten Uncensorable Years, or How Liver-sausage Lost its Political Implications STANISLAW BARAŃCZAK	page 97
19–500 Goldap ANKA KOWALSKA	108
The Last Time I Went to Press VICTOR NEKRASOV	110
The Censor IVAN KRAUS	114
A Cup of Coffee with My Interrogator LUDVÍK VACULÍK	116
Slit Lips SAMIH AL-QASIM	124
Dr Azudi, the Professional REZA BARAHENI	125
Eyewitness to Death MUZAFFER ERDOST	126
Stop the Lie SIPHO SEPAMLA	132
A Writer's Freedom NADINE GORDIMER	134
For a Cent DON MATTERA	141
The Failure of Censorship ANDRÉ BRINK	142
Comedy is Everywhere MILAN KUNDERA	150
You Have Insulted Me: a Letter KURT VONNEGUT	157
The Writer in Latin America MARIO VARGAS LLOSA	161
Something More than Words JULIO CORTÁZAR	172
Witness in Difficult Times RODOLFO WALSH	180

| Contents | 7 |

Last Will and Testament ARIEL DORFMAN	*page* 186
In Defence of the Word EDUARDO GALEANO	188
Index on Censorship	200

Acknowledgements

For permission to reprint copyright material, the editor and publishers gratefully acknowledge the following: Delacorte Press/Seymour Lawrence and Jonathan Cape Ltd for an extract from *Palm Sunday* by Kurt Vonnegut, Copyright © 1981 by the Ramjac Corporation; Heinemann Educational Books Ltd for an extract from *Detained: A Writer's Prison Diary* by Ngũgĩ wa Thiong'o; Palach Press for 'A Cup of Coffee with My Interrogator' by Ludvík Vaculík; *Staffrider* magazine and Ravan Press (Pty) Ltd for 'Stop the Lie' by Sipho Sepamla; and the many other publishers, writers and translators who have contributed to this collection.

Note on the illustrations: 8 cartoons by Maris Bishofs. Maris Bishofs is a Latvian cartoonist who left the USSR with his Jewish wife in 1972. He is now living in Long Island city and his work appears regularly in the *Washington Post*, the *New York Times*, the *Atlantic* and *Village Voice*.

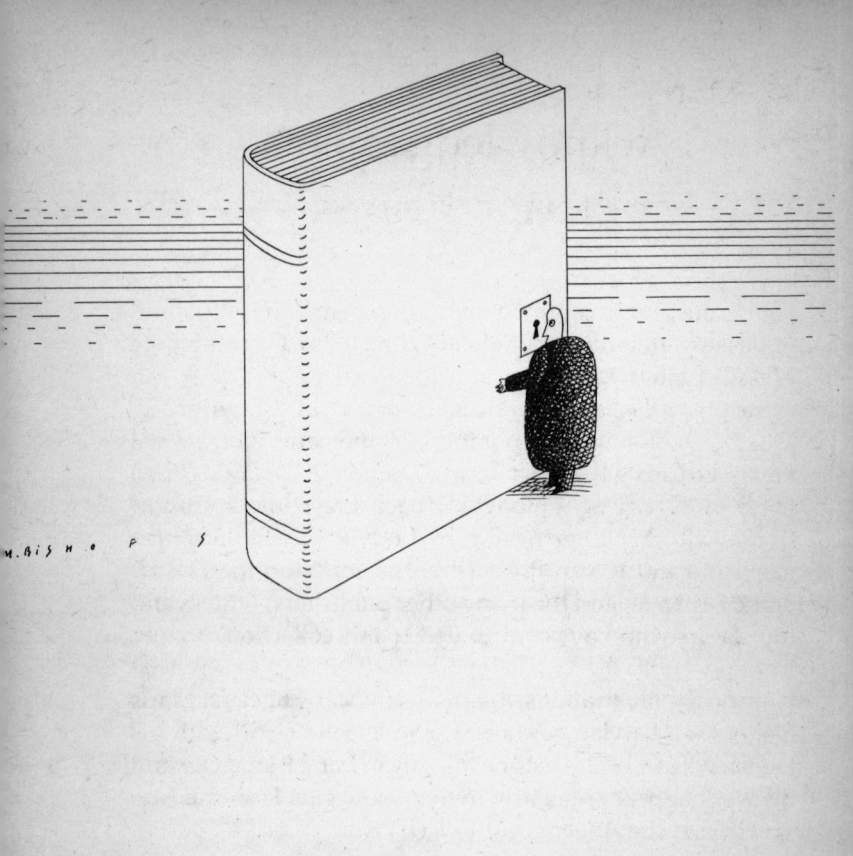

Introduction
GEORGE THEINER

In the midst of the farewells and the crimes, will words survive?
Eduardo Galeano

A middle-aged Russian novelist, holder of the Stalin Prize for Literature, and a young Polish poet; a leading South African writer, and a recently deceased Turkish publisher; a young Chinese, who at fifteen was a fanatical Red Guard, and a distinguished Greek lawyer, now the Minister of Justice in the government of Andreas Papandreou; a well-known Argentinian investigative journalist, and a Czech poet living in exile in Paris. . . .

What can these eight people have in common?

Their stories, or examples of their work, have appeared in the pages of *Index on Censorship* over the past twelve years, as they have all been the victims of repression and persecution by dictatorial regimes of one shade or another. The publisher, Ilhan Erdost, was killed while under military escort in Ankara in November 1980; Rodolfo Walsh, the Argentinian journalist, 'disappeared' from his home in Buenos Aires in March 1977 and has not been heard of since. Professor George Mangakis was sentenced to fourteen years' imprisonment during the reign of the Greek colonels, while Wei Jingsheng is at present serving fifteen years in communist China. The Russian, Polish and Czech writers —Victor Nekrasov, Stanisław Barańczak, Jan Vladislav— are all involuntary exiles in the West.

I have chosen the eight at random from the authors represented in this volume; and they again are only a fraction of the people whose fate has been reported in the magazine and whose banned work has been published in it. The Writers in Prison Committee of International PEN has on its books today a total of 480 novelists, poets and other authors who are languishing in prison or labour camp somewhere in the world, who have 'disappeared' or are interned in psychiatric hospitals.

But a writer does not have to be incarcerated in a prison cell or a psychiatric ward, he does not have to be abducted or murdered, to be silenced by a regime which does not approve of him. To be banned, censored, unable to publish his work can, to a dedicated writer, be a 'fate worse than death'—and it is a fate that is shared by thousands in every part of the globe.

It was to help banned, censored and persecuted writers, whatever their nationality, colour, religious creed or political persuasion, that *Index on Censorship* came into being in 1972. To help them by alerting the public to their fate and by giving them the satisfaction of seeing at least a small sample of their output in print. How important this can be is best illustrated by the case of Don Mattera, a South African journalist and poet whose circumscribed existence as a 'banned' person in the early seventies depressed him so much that, as he has told us, he stopped writing poetry. But when, a year or two later, he learned that six of his poems had appeared in *Index* he felt that all was not lost and, thus encouraged, started writing poetry again.

Don Mattera's story is one of the happier ones among the proscribed writers of the world, for his banning order was unexpectedly lifted last year and he can now be published not only abroad but also in his own country.

Those who cannot, lead a strange, shadowy existence. They become true 'non-persons' in George Orwell's famous phrase, their literary efforts circulating, at best, in typescript copies, all their earlier books removed from public libraries, their very names never mentioned in the official media, their entries in writers' *Who's Who* obliterated, as was Victor

Nekrasov's from the *Soviet Encyclopedia* twelve years ago. This famous Russian novelist and holder of the Stalin Prize for Literature fell from grace for his courageous defence of Alexander Solzhenitsyn and other dissidents.

There are, of course, many forms of censorship. The extreme form, as George Bernard Shaw put it, is assassination—a favourite method of dealing with obstreperous writers in Idi Amin's Uganda as well as in a number of Latin American countries. Nearer home, Hitler and Stalin cut short many a writer's career by similar means. Writers killed, their books banned, sometimes burned in public as were those of Thomas Mann and other leading German writers by a Nazi mob in Berlin in 1933—in a backhanded sort of way, their treatment by so many totalitarian (and sometimes even non-totalitarian) regimes can be considered a compliment to the author and his craft. Is the writer really that important?

'All that a writer can do is to go on writing the truth as he sees it,' said Nadine Gordimer in a speech she gave at a conference in Durban in 1975. And in those few simple words perhaps lies the answer to my question. The truth is often unwelcome, it can upset the worn-out old apple-cart of lies and official propaganda peddled by the regime's loyal hacks. Or it can point an accusing finger at some of the people at the top, sometimes at Big Brother himself. Why else would the Bulgarian writer and broadcaster Georgi Markov have been sent to an untimely end on Waterloo Bridge in a manner that belongs to the annals of James Bond rather than to real life?

There are many forms of censorship. And, while not forgetting how fortunate we are to be living (and writing) in a part of the world where writers are free from the fear of a nocturnal visit by the secret police, where they are not declared 'banned' persons and where their work does not have to be done, in the descriptive Czech phrase, 'for the drawer'—we nevertheless should not give way to self-congratulation and complacency. Even the most liberal of governments (as governments go) can be surprisingly illiberal on occasion. After all, the *Lady Chatterley* trial did not take place in an East European dictatorship nor in a newly independent African state.

The *Lady Chatterley* case ended in a victory for common sense and for literature. And it happened all of three decades ago. But that is not to say that literary creation in this or any country is free from threat—a threat that does not always come from governments. Indeed, in the democracies of Western Europe and North America it is far more likely to come from unofficial groups of self-appointed censors and guardians of our moral welfare, as witness the case of Kurt Vonnegut's *Slaughterhouse Five*, which was consigned to the flames of the school furnace in Drake, North Dakota, by decision of the school board and its chairman, Mr Charles McCarthy. An unfortunate coincidence of names, but it is not the name of the chairman which makes this such a deplorable incident.

Vonnegut's book was described by the school board as 'unwholesome', and the janitor was therefore given instructions to burn it. Even by the standards of Queen Victoria, commented the author, the only offensive line in the novel was 'Get out of the road, you dumb motherfucker', spoken by a GI during the Battle of the Bulge in 1944.

What is even more shocking than this single incident which took place ten years ago is the 'league table' of works by leading American writers which have been most frequently removed from the curriculum of US schools or from the shelves of school libraries between the years 1966 and 1975. They include Salinger's *Catcher in the Rye*, Heller's *Catch 22*, Harper Lee's *To Kill a Mockingbird*, two novels by John Steinbeck (*The Grapes of Wrath* and *Of Mice and Men*) and our old friend *Slaughterhouse Five*.

'Unwholesome' books, unwelcome criticism, unsuitable authors—unsuitable because they are of the wrong colour or race, because they do not toe the party line, because they try to write the truth as they see it—all these will sooner or later find their way to the pages of *Index on Censorship*. Some of them may attract the attention of a British or American publisher, even though their work cannot be published in their own language.

One London publisher whose list includes several distinguished *Index* 'clients' is Faber & Faber. I should like to take this opportunity to thank Faber for giving us the chance to bring some of these authors and the problem of censorship to a wider readership. Thanks are also due to the Palestinian poet Samih al-Qasim, who provided us with the title, and above all to the writers whose work appears in this book. We regret that in the interests of space-saving we have not been able to reproduce all of the pieces in full: those who would like to read uncut texts may obtain them from the offices of *Index on Censorship*.

Note
STEPHEN SPENDER

Reading this collection of writings by men and women who have, in their countries of origin, suffered various forms and degrees of persecution—all of them forms of censorship—the reader living in that world of comparative freedom which is misnamed 'the West', may be tempted to feel that all this has nothing to do with him. These writers and their works, he may think, belong to some order of humanity different from that which he inhabits. For him to read their work is a kind of spiritual or literary slumming.

There are reasons, however, why these essays, poems and reports should be very much our concern. The most obvious one is that their situation might very well one day be ours. These are the documents of a day that may be our tomorrow. The least of their merits is that they serve as warnings. A far more important reason is that they are about extreme situations—imprisonment, deprivation, violent death—within the whole human condition of the world in our time which tell us realities about our own lives as well as those of these victims. For we all belong to the life of our time wherever it is happening. Despite the views of ideologists we are none of us creatures of the political systems in which we live. We are all of us human beings, individuals. What happens to individuals over there, living in their world of totalitarian dictatorships (taking different forms in different countries) tells us something about what is happening to us ourselves. For we are all dimly aware that on some level of our consciousness what happens to people in concentration camps and prisons, happens also to us.

The most imaginative of the writers here present to us in their work that 'naked humanity' which Lear saw in the plight of Edgar feigning madness on the stormy heath. They themselves, living under oppression, are brought up against fundamental problems of the values of life and of religion which it is difficult for us to see in our world of advertising and much spiritual confusion. By a very ironic paradox, they are even recognized by the governments that censor them as a political force, in a way in which writers are not recognized in our democracies. That they tell their own truth constitutes a danger to the regime and is a sufficient reason for censoring them. They write about the actual condition of the minds and bodies of human beings living under authoritarian governments which, with their police, their bureaucracy and their propaganda, are dehumanizing. Most of all, we can learn from them to reflect on the uses to which we put our own freedoms.

How *Index on Censorship* Started
MICHAEL SCAMMELL

Michael Scammell was the editor of Index on Censorship *from 1972 to August 1980. This article appeared in 1981.*

Starting a magazine is as haphazard and uncertain a business as starting a book—who knows what combination of external events and subjective ideas has triggered the mind to move in a particular direction? And who knows, when starting, whether the thing will work or not and what relation the finished object will bear to one's initial concept? That, at least, was my experience with *Index*, which seemed almost to invent itself at the time and was certainly not 'planned' in any rational way. Yet looking back, it is easy enough to trace the various influences that brought it into existence.

It all began in January 1968 when Pavel Litvinov, grandson of the former Soviet Foreign Minister, Maxim Litvinov, and his English wife, Ivy, and Larisa Bogoraz, the former wife of the writer, Yuli Daniel, addressed an appeal to world public opinion to condemn the rigged trial of two young writers and their typists on charges of 'anti-Soviet agitation and propaganda' (one of the writers, Alexander Ginzburg, was released from the labour camps in 1979 and now lives in Paris: the other, Yuri Galanskov, died in a camp in 1972). The appeal was published in *The Times* on 13 January 1968 and evoked an answering telegram of support and sympathy from sixteen English and American luminaries, including W. H. Auden, A. J. Ayer, Maurice Bowra, Julian Huxley, Mary McCarthy, Bertrand Russell and Igor Stravinsky.

The telegram had been organized and dispatched by

Stephen Spender and was answered, after taking eight months to reach its addressees, by a further letter from Litvinov, who said in part: 'You write that you are ready to help us "by any method that is open to you". We immediately accepted this not as a purely rhetorical phrase, but as a genuine wish to help. . . .' and went on to indicate the kind of help he had in mind:

> My friends and I think it would be very important to create an international committee or council that would make it its purpose to support the democratic movement in the USSR. This committee could be composed of universally respected progressive writers, scholars, artists and public personalities from England, the United States, France, Germany and other western countries, and also from Latin America, Asia, Africa and, in the future, even from Eastern Europe . . . Of course, this committee should not have an anti-communist or anti-Soviet character. It would even be good if it contained people persecuted in their own countries for pro-communist or independent views. . . . The point is not that this or that ideology is not correct, but that it must not use force to demonstrate its correctness.

Stephen Spender took up this idea first with Stuart Hampshire (the Oxford philosopher), a co-signatory of the telegram, and with David Astor (then editor of the *Observer*), who joined them in setting up a committee along the lines suggested by Litvinov (among its other members were Louis Blom-Cooper, Edward Crankshaw, Lord Gardiner, Elizabeth Longford and Sir Roland Penrose, and its patrons included Dame Peggy Ashcroft, Sir Peter Medawar, Henry Moore, Iris Murdoch, Sir Michael Tippett and Angus Wilson). It was not, admittedly, as international as Litvinov had suggested, but it was thought more practical to begin locally, so to speak, and to see whether or not there was something in it before expanding further. Nevertheless, the chosen name for the new organization, Writers and Scholars International, was an earnest of its intentions, while its deliberate echo of Amnesty International (then relatively modest in size) indicated a feeling that not only literature, but also human rights would be at issue.

By now it was 1971 and in the spring of that year the committee advertised for a director, held a series of interviews and offered me the job. There was no programme, other than Litvinov's letter, there were no premises or staff, and there was very little money, but there were high hopes and enthusiasm.

It was at this point that some of the subjective factors I mentioned earlier began to come into play. Litvinov's letter had indicated two possible forms of action. One was the launching of protests and appeals to 'support and defend' people who were being persecuted for their civic and literary activities in the USSR. The other was to 'provide information to world public opinion' about this state of affairs and to operate with 'some sort of publishing house'. The temptation was to go for the first, particularly since Amnesty was setting such a powerful example, but precisely because Amnesty (and the International PEN Club) were doing such a good job already, I felt that the second option would be the more original and interesting to try. Furthermore, I knew that two of our most active members, Stephen Spender and Stuart Hampshire, on the rebound from *Encounter* after disclosures of CIA funding, had attempted unsuccessfully to start a new magazine, and I felt that they would support something in the publishing line. And finally, my own interests lay mainly in that direction. My experience had been in teaching, writing, translating and broadcasting. Psychologically I was too much of a shrinking violet to enjoy kicking up a fuss in public. I preferred argument and debate to categorical statements and protest, the printed page to the soapbox; I needed to know much more about censorship and human rights before having strong views of my own.

At that stage I was thinking in terms of trying to start some sort of alternative or 'underground' (as the term was misleadingly used) newspaper—*Oz* and the *International Times* were setting the pace in those days, with *Time Out* just in its infancy. But a series of happy accidents began to put other sorts of material into my hands. I had been working recently on Solzhenitsyn and suddenly acquired a tape-recording with some unpublished poems in prose on it. On a visit to Yugoslavia I called on Milovan Djilas and was unexpectedly offered some of his short stories. A Portuguese writer living in London, José Cardoso Pires, had just written a first-rate essay on censorship that fell into my hands. My friend, Daniel Weissbort, editor of *Modern Poetry in Translation*, was working on some fine lyrical poems by the Soviet poet, Natalya Gorbanevskaya, then in a mental hospital. And above all I stumbled across the magnificent 'Letter to Europeans' by the Greek law professor, George Mangakis, written in one of the colonels' jails (which I still consider to be one of the best things I have ever published). It was clear that these things wouldn't fit very easily into an *Oz* or *International Times*, yet it was even clearer that they reflected my true tastes and were the kind of writing, for better or worse, that aroused my enthusiasm. At the same time I discovered that from the point of view of production and editorial expenses, it would be far easier to produce a magazine appearing at infrequent intervals, albeit a fat one, than to produce even the same amount of material in weekly or fortnightly instalments in the form of a newspaper. And I also discovered, as Anthony Howard put it in an article about the *New Statesman*, that whereas opinions come cheap, facts tend to come dear, and facts were essential in an explosive field like human rights. Somewhat thankfully, therefore, my one assistant and I settled for a quarterly magazine.

There is no point, I think, in detailing our sometimes farcical discussions of a possible title. We settled on *Index* (my suggestion) for what seemed like several good reasons: it was short; it recalled the Catholic *Index Librorum Prohibitorum*; it was to be an index of violations of intellectual freedom; and lastly, so help me, an index finger pointing accusingly at the guilty oppressors—we even introduced a graphic of a pointing finger into our early issues. Alas, when we printed our first covers bearing the bold name of *Index* (vertically, to attract attention) nobody got the point (pun unintended). Panicking, we hastily added the words 'on censorship' as a subtitle—*Censorship* had been the title of an earlier magazine, by then defunct—and this it has remained ever since, nagging me with its ungrammaticality (index *of* censorship, surely) and a standing apology for the opacity of its title. I have since come to the conclusion that it is a thoroughly bad title—Americans, in particular, invariably associate it with the cost of living and librarians with, well, indexes. But it is too late to change now.

Our first issue duly appeared in May 1972, with a programmatic article by Stephen Spender (printed also in the *TLS*) and some cautious 'Notes' by myself. Stephen summarized some of the events leading up to the foundation of the magazine (not naming Litvinov, who was then in exile in Siberia) and took freedom and tyranny as his theme:

> Obviously there is the risk of a magazine of this kind becoming a bulletin of frustration. However, the material by writers which is censored in Eastern Europe, Greece, South Africa and other countries is among the most exciting that is being written today. Moreover, the question of censorship has become a matter of impassioned debate; and it is one which does not only concern totalitarian societies.

I contented myself with explaining why there would be no formal programme and emphasized that we would be feeling our way step by step. 'We are naturally of the opinion that a definite need [for us] exists. . . . But only time can tell whether the need is temporary or permanent —and whether or not we shall be capable of satisfying it. Meanwhile our aims and intentions are best judged . . . by our contents, rather than by editorials.'

In the course of the next few years it became clear that the need for such a magazine was, if anything, greater than I had foreseen. The censorship, banning and exile of writers and journalists (not to speak of imprisonment, torture and murder) had become commonplace, and it seemed at times that if *we* hadn't started *Index*, someone else would have, or at least something like it. And once the demand for censored literature and information about censorship was made explicit, the supply turned out to be copious and inexhaustible.

One result of being inundated with so much material was that I quickly learned the geography of censorship. Of course, in the ten years since *Index* began there have been many changes. Greece, Spain and Portugal are no longer the dictatorships they were then. There have been major upheavals in Poland, Turkey, Iran, the Lebanon, Pakistan, Nigeria, Ghana and Zimbabwe. Vietnam, Cambodia and Afghanistan have been silenced, whereas Chinese writers have begun to find their voices again. In Latin America Brazil has attained a measure of freedom, but the southern cone countries of Chile, Argentina, Uruguay and Bolivia have improved only marginally and Central America has been plunged into bloodshed and violence.

Despite the changes, however, it became possible to discern enduring patterns. The Soviet empire, for instance, continued to maltreat its writers throughout the period of my editorship. Not only was the censorship there highly organized and rigidly enforced, but writers were arrested, tried and sent to jail or labour camps with monotonous regularity. At the same time, many of the better ones, starting with Solzhenitsyn, were forced or pushed into exile, so that the roll-call of Russian writers outside the Soviet Union (Solzhenitsyn, Sinyavsky, Brodsky, Zinoviev, Maximov, Voinovich, Aksyonov, to name but a few) now more than rivals, in talent and achievement, those left at home. Moreover, a whole array of literary magazines, newspapers and publishing houses has come into existence abroad to serve them and their readers.

In another main black spot, Latin America, the censorship tended to be somewhat looser and ill-defined, though backed by a campaign of physical violence and terror that had no parallel anywhere else. Perhaps the worst were Argentina and Uruguay, where dozens of writers were arrested and ill-treated or simply disappeared without trace. Chile, despite its notoriety, had a marginally better record with writers, as did Brazil, though the latter had been very bad during the early years of *Index*.

In other parts of the world, the picture naturally varies. In Africa, dissident writers are often helped by being part of an Anglophone or Francophone culture. Thus Wole Soyinka was able to leave Nigeria for England, Kofi Awoonor to go from Ghana to the United States (though both were temporarily jailed on their return), and French-speaking Camara Laye to move from Guinea to neighbouring Senegal. But the situation can be more complicated when African writers turn to the vernacular. Ngũgĩ wa Thiong'o, who has written some impressive novels in English, was jailed in Kenya only after he had written and produced a play in his native Gikuyu.

In Asia the options also tend to be restricted. A mainland Chinese writer might take refuge in Hong Kong or Taiwan, but where is a Taiwanese to go? In Vietnam, Cambodia, Laos, the possibilities for exile are strictly limited, though many have gone to the former colonizing country, France, which they still regard as a spiritual home, and others to the USA. Similarly, Indonesian writers still tend to turn to Holland, Malaysians to Britain, and Filipinos to the USA.

In documenting these changes and movements, *Index* was able to play its small part. It was one of the very first magazines to denounce the Shah's Iran, publishing as early as 1974 an article by Sadeq Qotbzadeh, later to become Foreign Minister in Ayatollah Khomeini's first administration. In 1976 we publicized the case of the tortured Iranian poet, Reza Baraheni, whose testimony subsequently appeared on the op-ed page of the *New York Times*. (Reza Baraheni was arrested, together with many other writers, by the Khomeini regime on 19 October 1981.) One year later, *Index* became the publisher of the unofficial and banned Polish journal, *Zapis*, mouthpiece of the writers and intellectuals who paved the way for the present liberalization in Poland. And not long after that it started putting out the Czech unofficial journal, *Spektrum*, with a similar intellectual programme. We also published the distinguished Nicaraguan poet, Ernesto Cardenal, before he became Minister of Education in the revolutionary government, and the South Korean poet, Kim Chi-ha, before he became an international *cause célèbre*.

One of the bonuses of doing this type of work has been the contact, and in some cases friendship, established with outstanding writers who have been in trouble: Solzhenitsyn, Djilas, Havel, Barańczak, Soyinka, Galeano, Onetti, and with the many distinguished writers from other parts of the world who have gone out of their way to help: Heinrich Böll, Mario Vargas Llosa, Stephen Spender, Tom Stoppard, Philip Roth—and many others too numerous to mention. There is a kind of global consciousness coming into existence, which *Index* has helped to foster and which is especially noticeable among writers. Fewer and fewer are prepared to stand aside and remain silent while their fellows are persecuted. If they have taught us nothing else, the Holocaust and the Gulag have rubbed in the fact that silence can also be a crime.

The chief beneficiaries of this new awareness have not

been just the celebrated victims mentioned above. There is, after all, an aristocracy of talent that somehow succeeds in jumping all the barriers. More difficult to help, because unassisted by fame, are writers perhaps of the second or third rank, or young writers still on their way up. It is precisely here that *Index* has been at its best.

Such writers are customarily picked on, since governments dislike the opprobrium that attends the persecution of famous names, yet even this is growing more difficult for them. As the Lithuanian theatre director, Jonas Jurasas, once wrote to me after the publication of his open letter in *Index*, such publicity 'deprives the oppressors of free thought of the opportunity of settling accounts with dissenters in secret' and 'bears witness to the solidarity of artists throughout the world'.

Looking back, not only over the brief ten years since *Index* was started, but much further, over the history of our civilization, one cannot help but realize that censorship is by no means a recent phenomenon. On the contrary, literature and censorship have been inseparable pretty well since earliest times. Plato was the first prominent thinker to make out a respectable case for it, recommending that undesirable poets be turned away from the city gates, and we may suppose that the minstrels and minnesingers of yore stood to be driven from the castle if their songs displeased their masters. The examples of Ovid and Dante remind us that another old way of dealing with bad news was exile: if you didn't wish to stop the poet's mouth or cover your ears, the simplest solution was to place the source out of hearing. Later came the Inquisition, after which imprisonment, torture and execution became almost an occupational hazard for writers, and it is only in comparatively recent times—since the eighteenth century—that scribblers have fought back and demanded an unconditional right to say what they please. Needless to say, their demands have rarely and in few places been met, but their rebellion has resulted in a new psychological relationship between rulers and ruled.

Index, of course, ranged itself from the very first on the side of the scribblers, seeking at all times to defend their rights and their interests. And I would like to think that its struggles and campaigns have borne some fruit. But this is something that can never be proved or disproved, and perhaps it is as well, for complacency and self-congratulation are the last things required of a journal on human rights. The time when the gates of Plato's city will be open to all is still a long way off. There are certainly many struggles and defeats still to come—as well, I hope, as occasional victories. When I look at the fragility of *Index*'s financial situation and the tiny resources at its disposal I feel surprised that it has managed to hold out for so long. No one quite expected it when we started. But when I look at the strength and ambitiousness of the forces ranged against it, I am more than ever convinced that we were right to begin *Index* in the first place, and that the need for it is as strong as ever. The next ten years, I feel, will prove even more eventful than the ten that have gone before.

God Keep Me from Going Mad
ALEXANDER SOLZHENITSYN

Alexander Solzhenitsyn, who was expelled from the Soviet Union in 1976 and now lives in Vermont, USA, wrote the following verses while serving a sentence in a labour camp in north Kazakhstan in 1950–3. They formed part of a longer, autobiographical poem and appeared in Index on Censorship *in 1972, the first publication in English of Solzhenitsyn's verse.*

God Keep Me from Going Mad

There never was, nor will be, a world of brightness!
A frozen footcloth is the scarf that binds my face.
Fights over porridge, the ganger's constant griping
And day follows day follows day, and no end to this dreary fate.

....

My feeble pick strikes sparks from the frozen earth.
And the sun stares down unblinking from the sky.
But the world *is* here! And will be! The daily round
Suffices. But man is not to be prisoned in the day.
To write! To write now, without delay,
Not in heated wrath, but with cool and clear understanding.
The millstones of my thoughts can hardly turn,
Too rare the flicker of light in my aching soul.
Yes, tight is the circle around us tautly drawn,
But my verses will burst their bonds and freely roam
And I can guard, perhaps, beyond their reach,
In rhythmic harmony this hard-won gift of speech.
And then they can grope my body in vain—
'Here I am. All yours. Look hard. Not a line . . .

Our indestructible memory, by wonder divine,
Is beyond the reach of your butcher's hands!'

My labour of love! Year after year with me you will grow,
Year after year you will tread the prisoner's path.
The day will come when you warm not me alone,
Nor me alone embrace with a shiver of wrath.
Let the stanzas throb—but no whisper let slip,
Let them hammer away—not a twitch of the lip,
Let your eyes not gleam in another's presence
And let no one see, let no one see
You put pencil to paper.
From every corner I am stalked by prison—
God keep me from going mad!*

I do not write my verses for idle pleasure,
Nor from a sense of energy to burn.
Nor out of mischief, to evade their searches,
Do I carry them past my captors in my brain.
The free flow of my verse is dearly bought,
I have paid a cruel price for my poet's rights:
The barren sacrifice of all her youth
And ten cold solitary years for my wife—

The unuttered cries of children still unborn,
My mother's death, toiling in gaunt starvation,
The madness of prison cells, midnight interrogations,
Autumn's sticky red clay in an opencast mine,
The secret, slow and silent erosive force
Of winters laying bricks, of summers feeding the furnace—
Oh, if this were but the sum of the price paid for my verse!
But those others paid the price with their lives,

*The first line of a poem by Pushkin.

God Keep Me from Going Mad

Immured in the silence of Solovki, drowned in thunder of waves,
Or shot without trial in Vorkuta's polar night.
Love and warmth and their executed cries
Have combined in my breast to carve
The receptive metre of this sorrowful tale,
These few poor thousand incapacious lines.
Oh, hopeless labour! Can you really pay the price?
Do you think to redeem the pledge with a single life?
For what an age has my country been so poor
In women's happy laughter, so very rich
In poets' lamentations!
Verse verse—for all that we have lost,
A drop of scented resin in the razed forest!
But this is all I live for! On its wings
I transport my feeble body through prison walls
And one day, in distant exile dim,
Biding my time, I will free my tortured memory from its thrall:
On paper, birchbark, in a blackened bottle rolled,
I will consign my tale to the forest leaves,
Or to a drift of shifting snow.

But what if beforehand they give me poisoned bread?
Or if darkness beclouds my mind at last?
Oh, let me die *there*! Let it not be here!
God keep me from going mad!

Translated by Michael Scammell

Letter to Europeans
GEORGE MANGAKIS

George Mangakis wrote his now famous 'Letter to Europeans' while in prison during the reign of the Greek Colonels. A Professor of Law at Salonica University, he was sentenced to eighteen years in 1969 but released three years later, when he was allowed to emigrate to West Germany. He lectured at Heidelberg until the fall of the Greek regime enabled him to return to Athens. He became Minister of Justice in the Papandreou Government. His 'Letter' was published in Index on Censorship *in 1972.*

The dimensions of my cell are approximately ten feet by ten feet. You gradually become accustomed to this space and even grow to like it, since, in a way, it is like a lair in which you lie hidden, licking your wounds. But in reality its object is to annihilate you. On one side of it there is a heavy iron door, with a little round hole in the upper part. Prisoners hate this little hole; they call it the 'stool pigeon'. It is through this hole that the jailer's eye appears every now and then—an isolated eye, without a face. There is also a peculiar lock, on the outside only; it locks with a dry, double sound. That is one thing you never get used to, no matter how much time goes by. It gives you the daily, tangible sensation of the violence that is being done to you. Before I came here, I didn't know that violence could be expressed so completely by the dry sound of a double lock.

On the other side of my cell there is a little window with bars. From this window you can see part of the city. And yet a prisoner rarely looks out of the window. It is too painful. The prisoner, of course, has a picture of life outside the prison constantly in his mind. But it is dim, colourless, like an old photograph; it is soft and shapeless. It is bearable. So you don't dare look out of the window. Its only use is to bring you some light. That is something I have studied very carefully. I have learned all the possible shades of light. I can distinguish the light that comes just before daybreak, and the light that lingers on after nightfall. This light, with its many variations, is one of the chief joys of the prisoner.

I live in this space, then, for endless hours of the day and night. It is like a piece of thread on which my days are strung and fall away, lifeless. This space can also be compared to a wrestling ring. Here a man struggles alone with the evil of the world.

I write these papers, and then I hide them. They let you write, but every so often they search your cell and take away your writings. They look them over, and after some time they return the ones which are considered permissible. You take them back, and suddenly you loathe them. This system is a diabolical device for annihilating your own soul. They want to make you see your thoughts through their eyes and control them yourself, from their point of view. It is like having a nail pushed into your mind, dislocating it. Against this method, which is meant to open up breaches in our defences and split our personality, there are two means of defence. First, we allow our jailers to take away *some* of our writings—the ones that express our views unequivocally. It is a way of provoking the jailers. We even derive a sort of childish satisfaction from thinking of the faces they'll make as they read. Then there are other papers which we prefer to hide—the ones we want to keep for ourselves.

There are moments when I sit in my cell thinking of what would be the best way to summarize my motives, those that made me end up in this cell and those that make me endure it. These motives are certainly not a belief in a single truth—not because we no longer have any truths to believe in but because, in our world, we do not experience these truths as absolute certainties. We are no longer as simple as that; we seek something more profound than certainty, something more substantial, something that is naturally, spontaneously simple. I think, then, that the totality of my motives in this connection could best be epitomized as hope—in other words, the most fragile, but also the most spontaneous and tenacious form of human thought. A deeply-rooted, indestructible hope, then, carved out the path that was to lead me, unrepentant, to this barren desert, and it is the same hope that makes me capable of enduring it, like those small, tormented desert plants which contain, inexplicably, two tiny drops of sap—drawn, I am sure, from their own substance. My hope is the equivalent of those two drops of sap. However, the intensity of my hope is equal to my difficulty in putting it into words. I might say, perhaps, that this hope concerns our humanity, which cannot be annihilated no matter how much it is persecuted on all sides; this is why there can be no purpose as serious, as noble, as to commit ourselves to its safeguard, even if we must inevitably suffer for it.

This hope takes shape only in certain attitudes. During the past months, through all the prisons I've known, I have often come across these attitudes. When I was held at the police station jails—those places of utter human degradation—I remember a girl who was locked in a cell next to mine. She had been there for five months. She hadn't seen the light of day once throughout that period. She had been accused of helping her fiancé to do Resistance work. At regular intervals, they would summon her for questioning and would try to make her disown him, using cunning persuasion or brutal intimidation alternately. If she disowned her fiancé, she would be set free. She refused unflinchingly, to the very end, even though she knew that her fiancé was dying of cancer and she would probably never see him again. He died on the day of her trial. She was a pale, frail girl, with a kind of nobility about her. Every evening she used to sing in her cell in a soft, low voice. She would sing till dawn about her love, in her sad voice. The girl's attitude is my hope. And so is the attitude of the doctor whom they tried to involve in our case. There was no evidence against him. If he had adopted a noncommittal attitude at the court martial he would certainly have been acquitted. But he was made of different mettle. When his turn came to take the stand at the trial, he got up and spoke about liberty. He defended liberty, even though he had a wife and children to support. He was sentenced to seven years in prison. What I would like to say here is quite simply this: in the attitude of people like that doctor and that girl, the dominant feeling is a spontaneous knowledge that the most important thing in life is to keep one's humanity. Because life does not belong to the barbarians, even when absolute authority does belong to them. Life belongs to human beings, life goes forward because of them. This is the source of my hope.

I live with a number of ideas that I love. They fill my days and nights. To the treacherous uniformity of my stagnant hours I oppose this dialogue with my ideas. Now I have come to know them better and to understand them better. I have actually experienced their significance. When I was being questioned, I discovered the essence of human dignity, in both its deepest and its simplest sense. When I was court-martialled I hungered for justice, and when I was imprisoned I thirsted for humanity. The brutal oppression which is now stifling my country has taught me a great deal, among other things the value of refusing to submit. As I sit in my cell thinking about these things, I am filled with a strange power—a power which has nothing in common with the power of my jailers. It is not expressed in a loud, insolent voice. It is the power of endurance—the power that is born of a sense of being right. That is how I face the relentless attack of empty days which has been launched against me. Each time, I repulse the attack at its very start. I begin my day by uttering the word 'freedom'. This usually happens at daybreak. I emerge from sleep, always feeling bitterly surprised to find myself in prison, as on the first day. Then I utter my beloved word, before the sense of being in prison has time to overpower me. This single word works like magic. And then I am reconciled to the new, empty day stretching ahead of me.

I often ask myself what it was exactly that touched our consciences in such a way as to give us all an imperatively personal motive for opposing the dictatorship and enlisting in the Resistance, putting aside all other personal obligations and pursuits. I keep thinking that this motive can be no other than the deep humiliation which the dictatorship represents for you, both as an individual and as a member of the people to whom you belong. When a dictatorship is imposed on your country, the very first thing you feel, the very first day, is humiliation. You are being deprived of the right to consider yourself worthy of responsibility for your own life and destiny. This feeling of humiliation grows day by day as a result of the oppressors' unceasing effort to force your mind to accept all the vulgarity which makes up the abortive mental world of dictators. You feel as if your reason and your human status were being deeply insulted every day. And then comes the attempt to impose on you, by fear, acceptance of their various barbarous actions—both those that you hear about and those that you actually see them commit against your fellow human beings. You begin to live with the daily humiliation of fear, and you begin to loathe yourself. And then, deeply wounded in your conscience as a citizen, you begin to feel a solidarity with the people to whom you belong. With a unique immediacy, you feel indivisibly bound to them and jointly responsible for their future fate. Thanks to this process of identification, you acquire an extraordinary historical acuity of vision, such as

Letter to Europeans

you had never known before, and you can see with total clarity that humiliated nations are inevitably led either to a lethal decadence, a moral and spiritual withering, or to a passion for revenge, which results in bloodshed and upheaval. A humiliated people either take their revenge or die a moral and spiritual death. Once you realize, then, the inevitability of your people's destruction, one way or another, your personal humiliation is turned into a sense of responsibility, and you don't simply join the Resistance, you become deeply committed to the Resistance. From that point onward, may God have mercy on you.

A lot of people don't understand us at all. It seems that it is difficult to understand an act that is motivated exclusively by the dictates of one's conscience, especially when the consequences of the act lead one to extreme situations. Our life is now based on values alone, not on interests. We have voluntarily placed ourselves in a position of unbearable suffering, and our main concern every day is not just to safeguard our humanity within this suffering, but to transmute this suffering into a component of our humanity. Upon our suffering we try to build a personality that excludes ordinary joys, the pursuit of happiness, and that is purely conceptual. We have become incarnated concepts. This means we do not live in the present. Besides, we have no days that we can call the present, except perhaps the days when our loved ones visit us. We exist as a result of the justification of our conscience, and for its sake alone. Thus there is no such thing as time for us. In this sense we could reach the absolute, if it weren't for the necessity to conquer this justification every day again from the very beginning. For this incarnation of abstract concepts is by no means a static condition; we still have blood in our veins, blood that pulsates with needs and desires, hearts that insist on dreaming, memories that ruminate on past happiness. We have our personal loves, for certain particular people. That is a constant threat to us. It means we have to struggle with ourselves in order to retain our conceptual condition, to balance ourselves upon the magnetic needle of conscience in its ceaseless quivering. Because of this constant effort, we are not absolute beings. Because of this effort, we are not yet dead.

Another thing: we feel very European. This feeling does not derive primarily from political opinions, even though it does end up by becoming a fundamental political stand. It is a feeling that grows out of the immediacy and the intensity that our cultural values have acquired under dictatorship. Fortunately, these values, which have become our whole life and which help us to endure our long nights and days, are not exclusively ours. We share them with all the peoples of Europe. Or rather the European people, for Europe is one single people. Here in prison we can affirm this with complete seriousness. Suffering helps us to get down to the essence of things and to express it with perfect simplicity. We see only the deeper meaning of Europe, not the foolish borders, the petty rivalries, the unfounded fears and reservations. We see ourselves simply as one people, as a whole. It may seem strange—though only at first glance—how intensely the Greeks felt they were Europeans the very first day of the dictatorship. Our values are the values of Europe. We created them together. We felt instinctively, at the time, that nobody but a European could understand the tragedy that was taking place in our country and feel about it the way we did. And we were right.

The headhunters have locked us up in this narrow place in order to make us shrink, like those hideous human scalps which are their trophies. But what they haven't realized is that our country was widened; it has become a whole continent. They have isolated us so as to turn us into solitary, forsaken creatures, lost in a purely individual fate. But we now live in the immense human community of

Letter to Europeans

European solidarity. Their power is helpless in the face of this knowledge.

We often talk about the dignity of man. It is not an abstraction; it is a thing which I have actually experienced. It exists in our very depths, like a sensitive steel spring. It has absolutely nothing to do with personal dignity. Its roots lie much deeper. Throughout the nightmare of the interrogation sessions, I lost my personal dignity; it was replaced by pure suffering. But human dignity was within me, without my knowing it. There came a moment when they touched it; the questioning had already been going on for some time. They cannot tell when this moment comes, and so they cannot plan their course accordingly. It functioned suddenly, like a hidden spring that made my scattered spiritual parts jerk upright, all of a piece. It wasn't really me who rose to my feet then, it was Everyman. The moment I began to feel this, I began to overcome the questioning ordeal. The effort was no longer only for myself. It was for all of us. Together we stood our ground.

I have experienced the fate of a victim. I have seen the torturer's face at close quarters. It was in a worse condition than my own bleeding, livid face. The torturer's face was distorted by a kind of twitching that had nothing human about it. He was in such a state of tension that he had an expression very similar to those we see on Chinese masks; I am not exaggerating. It is not an easy thing to torture people. It requires inner participation. In this situation, I turned out to be the lucky one. I was humiliated. I did not humiliate others. I was simply bearing a profoundly unhappy humanity in my aching entrails. Whereas the men who humiliate you must first humiliate the notion of humanity within themselves. Never mind if they strut around in their uniforms, swollen with the knowledge that they can control the suffering, sleeplessness, hunger, and despair of their fellow human beings, intoxicated with the power in their hands. Their intoxication is nothing other than the degradation of humanity. The ultimate degradation. They have had to pay very dearly for my torments. I wasn't the one in the worst position. I was simply a man who moaned because he was in great pain. I prefer that. At this moment I am deprived of the joy of seeing children going to school or playing in the parks. Whereas they have to look their own children in the face. It is their own humiliation that I cannot forgive the dictators.

One of the very few things I have been able to keep here is a picture of Erasmus. It's a newspaper clipping. I cut it out some time ago, and now I often look at it. It gives me a certain sense of peace. I suppose there must be some explanation for this. But I'm not interested in explanations. It is enough that there is this magic, this strange exaltation caused by the identification of this man with our own values, this victory over my solitude, which started centuries ago and which becomes real again as I look at his face. He is shown in profile. I like that. He is not looking at me, but he is telling me where to look. He reveals a solidarity of vision between us. In prison, this solidarity is a daily necessity, like the need for water, bread, sleep. When they search my cell they come upon Erasmus' picture, but they let me keep it. They don't understand. They've no idea how dangerous a mild, wise man can be. Sometimes I wonder about the jailer's eye, watching me through the hole in the door—where does *he* find solidarity of vision?

Our position as prisoners has many distinguishing features. One of them is that we sing, quite frequently. It may sound strange to people who don't know about prisons. Singing is part of the unwritten instructions passed on by veteran prisoners to newly arrived ones: when the pain and anguish are too much for you, sing. We begin to sing precisely when the anguish becomes unbearable. Singing seems to melt away that crushing burden we carry, just when we think we can no longer carry it; and then it rises out of us like an invisible grey mist. We feel a kind of relief. *They* know this, and that is why in some prisons, the harshest ones, singing is forbidden. I often sing in my cell, or I whistle. In this place singing is a real, immediate need of the spirit. It is the daily bread of those who are struggling not to go insane. I have never heard my jailers singing. Most of their time they are busy digesting their food.

We are shut away in our individual cells. In one respect we are the most helpless of creatures. They can do what they like with us. Just as we are sitting in our cell, they march in, they take us away, we don't know where, to some other prison, far away. If it weren't for their strange fear of us, I might say that they look upon us as objects. But this fear of theirs keeps our human status intact, even in their eyes. Now these helpless creatures think of nothing else but the fate of mankind. When we are taken out of our cells and meet our fellow prisoners, that is what we talk about. That is our sole concern. Like so many others, we know the meaning of this yearning for freedom that is pulsating throughout the world. And we can discern, more clearly than ever before, the enemies of freedom. We tremble for the fate of this great country which we call Europe. We know that hope hangs upon Europe, and that is the reason why it is constantly threatened. We know that someday, inevitably, Europe will play her role. That is why we tremble for Europe's fate today. That is why Europe is the sole concern of people like us—the most helpless of creatures.

It has all become quite clear to me. It had to be this way. From the moment my country was humiliated, debased, it was inevitable that I should go underground. It was an inexorable spiritual imperative. My whole life had been leading me to that imperative. Since childhood, I was taught to gaze upon open horizons, to love the human face, to respect human problems, to honour free attitudes. At the time of the Second World War, I was an adolescent; I lived through the Resistance; it left its moral mark on me. Only I didn't know at the time how deep that mark was. It has now become clear that it was to be the most vital inspiration force in my life. At last I can explain many things that happened to me between then and now. And so when the dictatorship came, I was already committed to the Resistance, without knowing it. I was carrying my own fate within me. Nothing happened by chance, by coincidence. Only the details were accidental. Diabolically accidental. But the general direction, the orientation, was rooted securely within me. Therefore it is not by mistake that I now find myself in prison. It is quite right that I should be here. What is horribly wrong is that this prison should exist at all.

During the months when I was being interrogated, alone before those men with the multiple eyes of a spider—and the instincts of a spider—one night a policeman on guard smiled at me. At that moment, the policeman was all men to me. Four months later, when the representative of the International Red Cross walked into my cell, once again I saw all men in his friendly face. When one day they finally put me in a cell with another prisoner and he began to talk to me about the thing he loved most in life—sailing and fishing boats—this man too was all men to me. It is true, then, that there are situations in which each one of us represents all mankind. And it is the same with these papers: I have entrusted them to a poor Italian prisoner who has just been released and who was willing to try to smuggle them out for me. Through him I hope they will eventually reach you. That man again is all men to me. But I think it is time I finished. I have raised my hand, made a sign. And so we exist. We over here in prison, and you out there who agree with us. So: *Freedom my love.*

All You Need is a Typewriter
JAN VLADISLAV

Jan Vladislav, one of the many Czech writers who were silenced after the communist coup of 1948, is a poet, essayist and translator. Since 1968 his work has only been published in Prague samizdat; in the 1970s he himself produced a series of unofficial publications. He emigrated to France in 1981 and wrote this article for Index on Censorship *in 1983.*

Czech parallel culture is none too well known abroad. Some of its products are—the plays of Václav Havel, the *feuilletons* of Ludvík Vaculík, the novels of Bohumil Hrabal, Ivan Klíma or Alexander Kliment—but not its history and its significance. That is because people just don't know much about the recent history of Czechoslovakia in general, the history of Central and Eastern Europe in the last fifty years. This is mainly due to the official propaganda and censorship, which have systematically stressed certain things while suppressing others, so that you get a totally distorted picture of Czech affairs, particularly of our culture and the parallel culture of the last few decades.

Czechoslovak history since 1948 has been presented, in the main, as the history of the Communist Party and its government, its resolutions and congresses, even its show trials. Yet that is only the tip of the iceberg, with the life of the nation continuing underneath the surface. It is this hidden face of reality that our unofficial literature has aimed to portray.

The history which Czech samizdat has helped to rescue from oblivion is the history of the silent majority, of the nation which suffered a terrible defeat in February 1948 when the Communists took power. This silent people, deprived of its rights, has not, however, remained inactive all these years; it has played its part in the history of the last half century by refusing to accept certain things and thus forcing the authorities to adapt their tactics and their policies. And at various times the nation's representatives—especially the writers—have managed to make themselves heard. When, at the Writers Congress in 1956, writers who stood outside the official structures such as Jaroslav Seifert and František Hrubin made their critical speeches, demanding for instance the abolition of censorship, they helped to change the course of events in the country. Similarly in Hungary and Poland, it was the writers and other intellectuals who were in the forefront of efforts to achieve change and reform, until finally the people as a whole could express their feelings and force their leaders to alter course.

In Czechoslovakia, and in particular in Bohemia, this happened towards the end of the 1950s, and of course even more markedly in 1968, and then again some ten years later with the appearance of Charter 77. This human rights movement brought together members of the older generation, who had been active in previous efforts at democratization, and many young people from the so-called musical underground.

It is the parallel culture, and in particular literature, which provides the most eloquent evidence of the nation's desire for freedom of expression. Literature plays such an important role because, purely for technical reasons, it is easy to produce. All you need is a typewriter, paper and some carbons, and you're in business. Manuscripts can be typed and circulated. It is less easy with other forms of artistic expression: you can't very easily make an unofficial film because for that you need a lot of equipment, and the same applies to the theatre.

This helps to explain why the regime takes such an inordinate interest in literature, seeing it as a dangerous adversary.

All You Need is a Typewriter

While unofficial literature came into its own in the 1970s, it has in reality far older roots. Many of the writers who are banned in Czechoslovakia today and can only publish in samizdat were already ousted from Czech literature during the Nazi occupation in 1939–45, and then again in the fifties. The communist authorities in 1948 disbanded the Writers Union and set up a new organization which simply excluded a large number of writers, including many respected and well-loved authors. These people were then for years prevented from publishing their work or playing any part in the life of the nation. The monopoly publishing houses created in the 1950s gave the regime yet another opportunity for weeding out the 'undesirables'.

Then came the political show trials in which some forty writers found themselves among the victims and were sentenced to long prison terms. One well-known writer and journalist, Záviš Kalandra, was sentenced to death and hanged. Those who were barred from publishing for many years included such top writers as Seifert and Holan. But it wasn't only our own Czech authors who got banned, countless foreign writers could likewise not be published. People like Baudelaire, Dostoyevsky, Rilke, Babel, not to mention Kafka and Orwell. All these became part of the samizdat network of unofficial literature in the 1950s.

The poet and artist Jiří Kolář is typical of those of us who were 'on the index' in those days. Between 1938 and 1958 he wrote twenty books of verse, yet to this day only six have been officially published. His poetry was widely circulated in samizdat, and when one of these volumes was discovered by the police during a house search, Kolář was arrested and sent to prison for a year. It was at this time that I first read the works of Josef Škvorecký—not only *The Cowards* which came out a little later officially only to cause a famous scandal and be withdrawn from sale, but also his *Tank Regiment* which has still not been published in Czechoslovakia except in samizdat.

All those collections of verse by Jiří Kolář have been circulating in typescript copies since the early seventies, and so have the books of Bohumil Hrabal. Although he *is* now being published in Prague, his popular novel *I Served the King of England* is still obtainable only on the black market in its samizdat edition.

Most of these banned writers were able to publish children's stories or translations of foreign literature. Jiří Kolář, Zdeněk Urbánek, Vladimír Holan, I myself devoted a great deal of time to translation, with the result that many fine works got published: Whitman, T. S. Eliot, Henri Michaux, Ungaretti, Mondale, and so on. Zdeněk Urbánek's new version of *Hamlet* was a milestone in our theatre, closely connected with the new direction taken by Czech drama itself thanks to authors such as Havel.

None of my books of essays or verse got into print, and when Vaculík brought out some of them in *Edice Petlice* ('Padlock Publications') in the seventies, he came to see me and expressed astonishment that I had written all this ten, twenty years previously. 'Why didn't you publish any of it?' he asked. 'Well,' I replied, 'because nobody was willing to take it.'

You asked what made me decide to start my own samizdat series, *Kvart* ('Quarto'). After the Soviet invasion of 1968, and in particular after 1970, the situation changed radically, so that many things which had been possible earlier—like proscribed authors publishing children's books, forewords, translations—were ruled out, as the regime learned its lesson and clamped down much more rigorously and consistently. The Writers Union, which had almost 800 members, was reduced to 120, some of the most prominent authors again finding themselves excluded. I am thinking of poets like Seifert and Holan, as well as Jiří Kolář, but also those who had, especially in the more liberal sixties, supported the regime—Vaculík, Klíma, Kohout and others. There was, of course, no question of people like Havel,

Kliment or myself being accepted for membership. We were all totally expelled from Czech literature.

The writers, however, had also learned from past experience. They realized that it wasn't enough to turn out the occasional typescript and they saw to it that Czech parallel culture in the seventies became better organized. In the West people imagine that we have clandestine printing shops, or at least use xerox machines and duplicators. All this is of course beyond the reach of the ordinary citizen, and should anyone manage to get hold of a duplicator, it would soon be confiscated. After all, the Husák regime has even taken away people's typewriters during police house searches.

Thus it was that some people started collecting unpublished manuscripts and approached other writers asking them to produce work, which they then had retyped in as many copies as possible. This usually meant a maximum of ten, or on electric typewriters fifteen, copies. In many cases there would then be a new 'printing' and these 'books' were bound in the normal way to make them more durable.

Padlock and the other samizdat series that sprang up in the early seventies couldn't handle everything, and in particular I felt that certain genres were being neglected. Essays, for example, or monographs on Kafka and Dostoyevsky, which my friends in Padlock handed over to me after I started *Kvart* in 1975.

Seifert was probably my most popular author. I must have brought out something like a thousand copies altogether, one 'printing' following another. He gave me his *Umbrella from Piccadilly* and said that was the final version. I put it out, but then he wrote two more poems and rearranged the collection, and so we had a new edition, and then several more. This was of course very useful for the author, as he could see his book as a whole and find out what the readers thought about it.

Translations form an important part of samizdat activity —books like Koestler's *Darkness at Noon*, the works of Hannah Arendt and Pierre Emmanuel, these were actually commissioned by the editors, who were able to build their own publication list.

Apart from Vaculík's Padlock and my own series, there were quite a few others: Havel's *Expedice* and other, smaller ones produced mainly by young people. Some of these specialized in poetry, some in prose, while various religious groups have their own series. These do not necessarily publish only religious literature to the exclusion of other genres—some very good philosophical works have been produced by them. The religious samizdat exists on a large scale and some of it is done quite professionally, even on duplicators and printing machines which other samizdat publishers do not possess. That is the reason for last year's large-scale police raids and arrests as well as the trial in Olomouc at which the organizers of this sort of unofficial publishing were sentenced to terms of imprisonment.

Coming back to my own series, it was not always easy to find the typists, as this work was very badly paid if it was paid at all. Often the typists would be volunteers, not professionals, and of course it showed. I also had to buy the necessary paper, and this had to be good-quality onion-skin and good carbon paper. And when everything had been typed and corrected I would bind the books myself, usually over the weekend because the police were less likely to visit then. It was a very difficult undertaking, you had to move the books from place to place and hide them in case you did get raided. Not that this activity was against the law—not even our law—but the police would nevertheless confiscate these things, and I couldn't afford to have that happen. At first I had my books bound by young professionals in binderies, but when this became too dangerous I bought some rather primitive equipment and became my own bookbinder. Of course there were problems, I didn't have a

All You Need is a Typewriter

guillotine and so had to trim everything by hand. Not to mention the problems of distribution, but friends helped out in this, as well as on the financial side.

When I later calculated it, I found that a book took on average ten days to produce. I mean ten full days of intensive work, reading and correcting typescripts, as well as manual work to do with binding. Apart from that there was a lot of travelling to be done, picking up manuscripts and delivering the finished product. When you take into account that I published 120 volumes, that makes 1200 working days, or three full years. Nobody can do this sort of thing all his life because you really must devote all your energies to it while you are doing it.

Then there are the non-literary problems involved. Once you start putting out any kind of samizdat, it does not take long for the police to become aware of it, and they will try to stop you any way they can. Since you are not really doing anything illegal, they resort to intimidation. Many a time I was either summoned or escorted to the police station, where they would ask me about my publishing activity. But I invariably refused to discuss it with them, repeating *ad infinitum* that I had no intention of discussing literary matters with the police. This infuriated them, but I insisted that the volumes we were producing would one day become part of the Czech literary heritage, if they weren't already. I gave examples of many works which had at one time or another been banned only to be accepted by the same regime a few years later. None of my publications was political—anything that was at all political I did not include in *Kvart* and brought out separately, but even these books could in no way be called subversive. Everything I did was in keeping with the Czechoslovak constitution and our laws, which allow freedom of expression.

The Security Police used devilish tactics in dealing with the publishers of samizdat. Some people got raided time and again. I was lucky and did not have a single house search. But during countless interrogations they said things like, 'Well, shall we pay you a visit and see what you've got at home?'—but they never did. Nevertheless, they managed to create an atmosphere of uncertainty, so that you never knew when it *might* happen.

During one such session they told me they would come and 'inspect your typewriter'. I said that if that's what they had in mind I couldn't very well stop them, and they started dictating for the record that I had agreed to the search. No, I don't agree, I told them, on the contrary I wish to protest against it, but there is nothing I can do to prevent it. And again they didn't come. Of course, there is always the possibility that they did pay us a visit when there was no one at home, but I had no means of knowing.

From the second half of 1979 they started taking an even greater interest in me. I got summoned practically every week, sometimes twice a week. Once they took me by car all the way to Benešov, and as often as not they would make veiled threats. And then not so veiled—I was actually threatened with physical violence. I know they do beat up people, so perhaps it was my age that saved me. But they did humiliate me and subjected me to body searches, though they had no legal right to do that.

All this lasted over a year, during which time they listened in to my telephone conversations, opened my mail, some of which then failed to reach me, confiscated my driving licence and forced me to retake my driving test several times, even though I had never had an accident, and the car was left standing outside the house for the best part of a year. My daughter, who lives in Canada and can visit Czechoslovakia, had her visa cancelled with the result that I did not see her or my grandchildren for ten years.

It became clear to me that sooner or later the police would create a situation that would enable them to have me locked up. And finally they started threatening my wife and tried to frame her on ordinary criminal charges such as theft. And so in the end I decided to leave the country. That is evidently what they had intended me to do, since my application to emigrate was dealt with in three days, whereas it normally takes people months and even years.

Do I regret having involved myself in unofficial publishing, which brought me all this unpleasantness and finally exile? No, not at all—on the contrary, I believe it was something I had to do. It was one way of preventing the Czech nation from being robbed of its identity and having an alien identity substituted instead. That I thought was very important, and I still do.

Translated by George Theiner

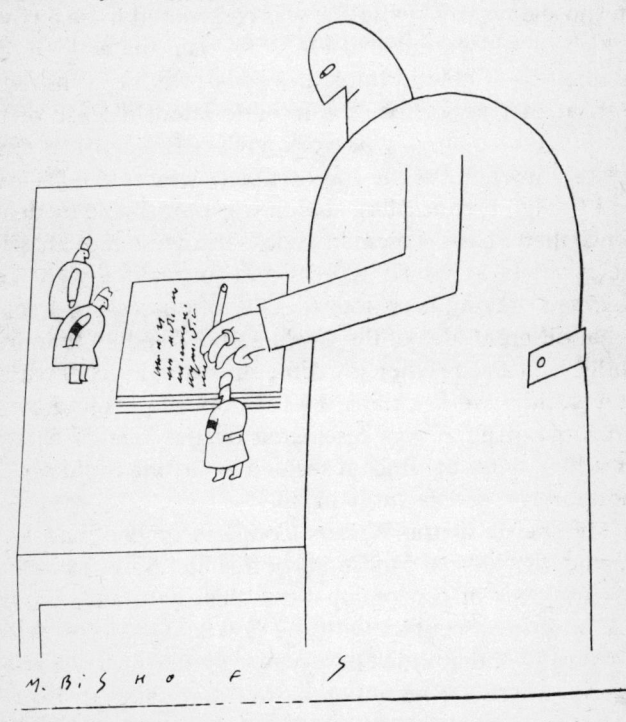

Variation on a Theme
IVAN KLÍMA

Ivan Klíma, a leading Czech novelist and short story writer, has been 'on the index' ever since the Soviet invasion of his country in 1968, his work appearing only in Prague samizdat and in translation abroad. The following piece was written for Index on Censorship *in 1981.*

I was born in Prague in the midst of a great economic crisis. In those days my birthplace was considered to be a city in which people were able to live as free men and women, that is, they were able to think and speak without hindrance. Yet, at that very time, the hitherto latent disease of our continent was already at work, eroding those freedoms. I was eight when Prague was occupied, when even listening to a foreign broadcasting station was punishable by death. Since then I have seen many books thrown out of libraries, many trials at which writers and journalists were condemned, having been found guilty of possessing a somewhat different idea of the world and of freedom than their judges. At an age when my contemporaries in other parts of the world were fascinated by the opposite sex and by sex and love itself, I was fascinated by the idea of external freedom, without which it seemed to me one could not live honourably, satisfactorily or fully.

My speech at the Writers Congress in 1967 had as its theme the external conditions of free literary work and the harmfulness of censorship—and this, naturally, brought me into direct conflict with the powers-that-were. And it was really at that time that my present fate as a writer first began, a writer who is not allowed to publish in his own country, whose books may not be sold, and whose manuscripts are confiscated by the police when they search his house.

There is no place on this earth where a man might be totally free. Nor can I imagine a force that would be capable of permanently depriving people of all freedom. Contemporary society cannot exist in complete freedom, nor can it exist in complete unfreedom.

Excessive external freedom which one happens to be born with, which is simply given to one without any effort on one's own part, no doubt has the same effect as any other excess: it tends to make us soft and leads to further excesses.

A lack of external freedom which one happens to be born with and which one can do nothing to change has the same effect as a shortage of anything else. It forces us to turn in upon ourselves. Just as the hungry man dreams about food and satiety appears to him to be the highest form of bliss, the man who is not free dreams of freedom, thinking that if only he could achieve it and obtain his proper rights, everything else would be at his fingertips. But it can happen that a man will only start thinking about what freedom means to him once he has lost it, and it can also happen that a man will unexpectedly gain external freedom: it is then that he discovers that this external freedom is no more than an opportunity, which may well show him his own emptiness, his unpreparedness for the free life he had been dreaming of.

It is generally accepted that an author cannot write in conditions of external unfreedom. Many times in this last decade I have been asked by visitors from abroad how I was able to bear my fate, how I could exist as a writer since I was not allowed to publish. These people have probably never asked themselves how did a writer exist who, while free to publish as and what he liked, actually had nothing to say, or for one reason or another desisted from saying it.

And so, as I have said, it is his inner freedom that really counts where an artist is concerned. He can live and work surrounded by brutality, he can live and work even though deprived of his rights. After all, the great Russian literature of the nineteenth century was created in one of the most unfree empires the world has ever known. Dostoyevsky was sentenced to death, and he lived in prisons and in exile. Solzhenitsyn conceived his works—at least in his mind — while serving time in the labour camps of Siberia. Many great works have only come to be published after the death of their authors. But no worthwhile work can be created by someone who lacks internal freedom.

What do I mean by internal freedom?

In one of his greatest novels, Karel Čapek tells the story of a railway employee who, just before his death, looks back on his 'Ordinary Life'. Suddenly he finds it full of missed opportunities, of other—sometimes better, nobler, more worthwhile, or again worse, pettier, less meaningful — lives. He had not lived any of them, the opportunities passed him by or they did not strike him as such at the time, or he saw them but backed away for lack of courage. 'He feared the voice that might have spoken to him.' Čapek here does not assess the validity of his hero's choices, rather he is interested in the fact that we all live only one of our many possible lives, and this is something common to us all — anyone else may seize the opportunity that was mine.

I would say that it is the man who knows how to choose, to detect his very own opportunity at every decisive turn in his life, who is truly internally free; he is not afraid of that voice, should it ever speak to him.

I start from the assumption that man is not a mere 'naked ape', not just one of the animal species living purely by their instincts but a being who has understood the reality of his own death and desires to overcome it, to continue when he has ceased to exist, to survive his earthly existence (whether we think of this as the posthumous existence of his soul or of his work, his *oeuvre*). It then seems to me that the way one lives may bring one closer to, or on the contrary alienate one from, this fundamental meaning of man's existence.

The internal freedom of each and every one of us will doubtless reveal itself in the way in which we are capable of discovering and maintaining this most fundamental aim of life, the way we again and again endeavour to keep faith with it, not allowing any external influence or pressure to divert us from it—whether this pressure takes the form of fashion, trend, convention, ideology, success, police terror, or the corrupting effect of fame and wealth.

I believe that in the course of the last few years I have learned to give up a great deal of what contemporary man considers to be a natural and even indispensable part of his everyday existence. By this I do not mean owning a passport, telephone, or the possibility to choose employment best suited to his abilities and training, nor am I thinking of the possibility to borrow in the library or to buy a book of one's own choosing—I have in mind the entire way of life as it is lived by artists and journalists in the cultured world: a life consisting of a variety of minor joys and worries such as the meetings of editorial and arts committees, lecture tours, the applause or otherwise of one's audience, study trips, letters from one's readers, press interviews, discussions with publishers, the experience brought by the success or failure of one's work, prizes, awards or other forms of public approval. At first it seemed to me that my life had been impoverished, yet as time went by I began to realize that, if anything, I had been freed from what I could call external ballast. The more I was deprived of things I had earlier cherished, the freer I felt; I was gradually becoming less vulnerable and more independent.

That is not to say that the road to freedom necessarily leads via some kind of asceticism. Nor would I claim that one has to come into conflict with the powers-that-be in order to gain internal freedom. No, all I am trying to say is that these two categories—external freedom, which allows one to accept all the joys and privileges (but also disadvantages) of modern life, and genuine internal freedom—have very little to do with one another.

Deprived of one's freedom of expression a man can easily lapse into despair, accept this unfreedom as his inevitable fate, fall silent and give up his soul to darkness—on the other hand, he can see this as a challenge. He may then discover that his earlier, more public, existence had been a form of escape from his own self, that while he was always ready to hold up a mirror to the world at large, he himself avoided looking in it or looked into a less harsh and critical one. And so today I believe that it is less important for a writer to worry about his freedom of expression than about what it is he wants to express. Or to put it another way: that he should at all times endeavour to express himself as a dignified, incorruptible and free human being.

Translated by George Theiner

Open Letter to President Husák
TOM STOPPARD

Tom Stoppard, the highly acclaimed British playwright, was refused admission to Czechoslovakia in 1981. Ironically, as he points out in this letter, he was born in Czechoslovakia; the family emigrated in 1938. This letter to President Husák appeared in Index on Censorship *in 1981.*

Dear President Husák,
I'm having a little trouble getting a visa to visit the CSSR and I wonder if you can help. It would be best of all if you helped me to get the visa, but it would be helpful if, failing that, you could tell me why I cannot have one. I spent a few enjoyable days in Prague some four years ago (my first return to your country since I emigrated in my mother's arms in 1938) and I have been looking forward to a return visit.

The first time I presented myself at the Czechoslovak consulate in London and filled in the appropriate form I was impressed by the ease and efficiency with which a visa was granted. When I tried again a couple of years later I was impressed only by the politeness of the gentleman who came to the counter to say, 'I am sorry, Mr Stoppard, but it is not desirable that you should receive a visa.'

Disarmed by this politeness I didn't like to embarrass him by asking him for any reason. Perhaps he would have replied that after my previous visit I had abused his country's hospitality by writing and speaking sympathetically about the Chartists. It did not seem to be the moment to start a philosophical discussion about human rights in general and Charter 77's objective in particular, namely the implementation of Czechoslovakia's admirable constitution. Instead, I retired from the field. Earlier this year I decided to have another go. My application for a visa was again refused without comment.

I should say that I think it is reasonable for any country to close its door against any person whom it would prefer to remain outside. I feel the same way about my house. Anybody who shows up at this address and criticizes my way of life and my moral values will not be asked back. I don't think that my behaviour in your house was particularly anti-social. Indeed, set against the virulence of the critics of government we shelter under our own roof, I would have thought that my conduct was genteel: a number of earnest discussions over cups of coffee, followed by an article of a few thousand words written in a tone which would have been far too mild to appeal to many of the newspapers and magazines which find themselves in weekly disagreement with the government over here. Be that as it may, I'm pretty sure that I have no 'human right' to enter your country if you don't want me to. So this letter is not to register a complaint, merely a disappointment. You have made your point: a visitor whose only anti-social intentions are to give token and pathetic moral support by drinking coffee and conversing with a handful of Chartists is not welcome.

Ought I to have left matters there? I had a sense of frustration. The occupational prejudice of playwrights is that things only move forward through dialogue. I also retain my faith, which may be an occupational naïvety, in progress through reason and reasonable discussion. So on 21 July 1981, I committed the naïve act of writing to Dr Němec, Minister of Justice for the Czechoslovak Republic, asking for an interview. Perhaps my visa application form, reduced to essential facts, carried with it an implication that I wished to run around Prague making all kinds of mischief. I suggested to Dr Němec that if someone could intercede on my behalf in this matter of a visa I would come to Prague, if necessary merely for one day, just to use up an hour of his time. I'll make no secret of the fact that at the back of my mind was the thought that in October my friend Václav Havel would be reaching the halfway point of his jail sentence and by Czech law, as I understand it, he would be eligible for parole. Frankly, Havel's prison sentence has been a great nuisance to me. Every week or so I have to ask myself what I can do to help him instead of being able to get on with my life and my work, so it would be a great relief if, after the failure of letters and telegrams, a personal word from the Minister himself settled the matter one way or another.

After five weeks without a response, I sent a telegram asking whether my letter had arrived. That was on 27 August. Seven weeks have passed. I rather think that I have now shot my bolt as regards achieving a return visit to Czechoslovakia.

And yet I am still troubled by a sense of incompleteness. Nothing that can be written or spoken is as ambiguous as silence, and I am troubled by this silence. I return to my work and to my life but at the back of my mind I ask myself whether this silence indicates a contemptuous indifference, a shiftiness, a tiny unease or a bureaucratic prudence. Perhaps it is not the endless silence which follows the last line of a dialogue, but merely a pause, a very long pause. I would still like to return to Prague, and this desire has become an end in itself, independent of any reason for going. Whether I go purely as a tourist for another look at the castle, whether I go to shake the hands of a few people who have fallen from grace and to reaffirm, uselessly, that they have not been entirely forgotten and ignored, or whether I go to have my bourgeois moral scruples corrected by someone in authority, the idea of going back, and the sense of frustration, remain with me. I have had no luck with official channels. Perhaps I'll have more luck with a sideways attempt: herewith, therefore, my final application for a visa to visit the Czechoslovak Socialist Republic.

Tom Stoppard,
October 1981

Free Thoughts on Toilet Paper
NGŨGĨ WA THIONG'O

Ngũgĩ wa Thiong'o, Kenya's best-known novelist and playwright, was until January 1978 chairman of the Literature Department of Nairobi University. On 6 January of that year he was detained 'for reasons of public security' and spent eleven months in detention before being released—but not reinstated. His plays in Gikuyu, performed by a rural community group, have been banned and since June 1982 Ngũgĩ has been living in Europe. The following is an extract from his prison diary, Detained: A Writer's Prison Diary *(Heinemann Educational Books, 1981).*

To hell with the warders! Away with intruding thoughts! Tonight I don't want to think about warders and prisoners, colonial or neo-colonial affairs. I am totally engrossed in the fictional heroine of the novel I have been writing on toilet paper for the last ten months or so!

Writing on toilet paper?

Now, I know: paper, any paper, is about the most precious article for a political prisoner, more so for one like me, who was in political detention because of his writing. For the urge to write is almost irresistible to a political prisoner. At Kamiti, virtually all the detainees are writers or composers. These prisoners have mostly written on toilet paper. Now the same good old toilet paper has enabled me to defy daily the intended detention of my mind.

Writing this novel has been a daily, almost hourly, assertion of my will to remain human and free despite the Kenya African National Union (KANU) official government programme of animal degradation of political prisoners.

Privacy, for instance. I mean its brutal invasion. Thus, I was daily trailed by a warder for twenty-four hours, in waking and sleeping. It was unnerving, truly unnerving, to find a warder watching me shit and urinate into a children's chamberpot in my cell, or to find him standing by the entrance to the toilet to watch me do the same exercise. The electric light is on the night long. To induce sleep, I had to tie a towel over my eyes. This ended in straining them so that after a month they started smarting and watering. But even more painful was to suddenly wake up in the middle of the night, from a dreamless slumber or one softened by sweet illusion or riddled with nightmares, to find two bodiless eyes fixed on me through the iron bars.

Or monotony: the human mind revolts against endless sameness. In ordinary social life, even the closest-knit family hardly ever spends a whole day together in meaningless circles on their compound. Man, woman and child go about their different activities in different places and they only meet in the evening to recount their different experiences. Experiments done on animals show that when they are confined to a small space and subjected to the same routines they end up tearing each other. Now the KANU Government was doing the same experiment on human beings.

At Kamiti, we daily saw the same faces in the same white *kuunguru* prison uniforms; we daily fed on *unga* and beans in the morning, at noon and at three o'clock; we daily went through the same motions, and this, in a confined space of reliefless dust and grey stones. The two most dominant colours in the detention block were white and grey and I am convinced these are the colours of death.

The government could not have been ignorant about the possible results of these experiments in mental torment: Valium was the most frequently prescribed drug in Kamiti Prison. The doctor expected a detainee to be mad or depressed unless proved otherwise.

A week after my incarceration. Wasonga Sijeyo, who had been in that block for nine years but had managed to keep a razor-sharp mind and a heart of steel, eluded the vigilant eyes of the warders then guarding me and within seconds he told me words that I came to treasure:

> It may sound a strange thing to say to you, but in a sense I am glad they brought you here. The other day—in fact a week or so before you came—we were saying that it would be a good thing for Kenya if more intellectuals were imprisoned. First, it would wake most of them from their illusions. And some of them might outlive jail to tell the world. The thing is . . . just watch your mind . . . don't let them break you and you'll be all right even if they keep you for life . . . but you must try . . . you have to, for us, for the ones you left behind.

Thus in addition to it being an insurrection of a detained intellect, writing this novel has been one way of keeping my mind and heart together like Sijeyo.

Free thoughts on toilet paper! I had deliberately given myself a difficult task. I had resolved to use a language which did not have a modern novel, a challenge to myself, and a way of affirming my faith in the possibilities of the languages of all the different Kenyan nationalities, languages whose development as vehicles for the Kenyan people's anti-imperialist struggles had been actively suppressed by the British colonial regime (1895–1963) and by the neo-colonial regime of Kenyatta and his comprador KANU cohorts. But content—not language and technique —would determine the eventual form of the novel. And the content? The Kenyan people's struggles against the neo-colonial form and stage of imperialism!

Easier said than done: where was I to get the inspiration? A writer needs people around him. He needs live struggles of active life. Contrary to popular mythology, a novel is not a product of the imaginative feats of a single individual but

Free Thoughts on Toilet Paper

the work of many hands and tongues. A writer just takes down notes dictated to him by life among the people, which he then arranges in this or that form. For me, in writing a novel, I love to hear the voices of the people working on the land, forging metal in a factory, telling anecdotes in crowded *matatus* and buses, gyrating their hips in a crowded bar before a jukebox or a live band, people playing games of love and hate and fear and glory in their struggle to live. I need to look at different people's faces, their gestures, their gait, their clothes, and to hear the variegated modulations of their voices in different moods. I need life to write about life.

But it is also true that nobody writes under circumstances chosen by him and on material invented by him. He can only seize the time to select from material handed to him by whomever and whatever is around him. So my case now: I had not chosen prison, I was forced into it, but now that I was there, I would try and turn the double-walled enclosure into a special school where, like Shakespeare's Richard II, I would study how I might compare: 'This prison where I live unto the world. . . .' In this literary target I was lucky to have for teachers, detainees and a few warders, who were very co-operative and generous in sharing their different mines of information and experience. Not only from conscious discussions and direct enquiries: whispered news of happenings outside the double walls would often provide me with material that I would later weave into the fabric of a novel.

In the daytime, I would take hasty notes on empty spaces of any book I might be reading, I would scribble notes on the bare walls of my cell, then in the evening I would try to put it all together on toilet paper.

Sometimes I would be seized with the usual literary boredom and despair—those painful moments when a writer begins to doubt the value of what he is scribbling or the possibility of ever completing the task in hand—those moments when a writer restrains himself with difficulty from setting the whole thing on fire, or tearing it all into pieces, or abandoning the whole project to dust and cobwebs. These moments are worse in prison because there are no distractions to massage the tired imagination: a glass of beer, a sound of music, or a long walk in sun and wind or in a starry night.

But at those very moments, I would remind myself that the KANU-led comprador ruling class had sent me here so that my brain would turn into a mess of rot. The defiance of this bestial purpose always charged me with new energy and determination: I would cheat them out of that last laugh by letting my imagination loose over the kind of society this class, in nakedly treacherous alliance with imperialist foreigners, was building in Kenya in total cynical disregard of the wishes of over 14 million Kenyans.

I am now on the last chapter. I have given myself 25 December as the deadline. 25 December 1978 has a special significance to me. In February or March I had told the other detainees that we would all 'eat' Christmas at home. I had even invited them to a Christmas goatmeat roasting party at my home. It was said half in joke, like so many other prison wagers related to dreams of eventual liberty, but I secretly believed it and inwardly clung to the date though becoming less and less openly assertive about it as days and nights rolled away. Now only twelve days are left. Twelve days to eat Christmas at home. Twelve days to meet my self-imposed literary deadline!

But tonight something else, an impulse, a voice, is urging me to run this last lap faster. The voice is not all that secret. Maybe it is born of the feverish expectation of early release which has been building up in the block for the last four months, though nobody is now sure of its 'ifs' and 'whens'. Maybe it is also born of a writer's usual excitement at seeing the light at the end of a long hazar-

Free Thoughts on Toilet Paper

dous tunnel. Or maybe it is a combination of both. But whatever its source, the voice remains insistent.

The heart is willing. The hand which has been scribbling non-stop since about seven o'clock is weak. But the voice is relentless: Write on!

Camara Laye—Involuntary Exile
DENIS HERBSTEIN

*Camara Laye (born Abdoulaye Camara) was a Guinean novelist who had to leave his homeland in 1964 and spent the next fifteen years in exile in neighbouring Senegal. Two of his books—*The African Child *and* The Radiance of the King—*have long been required reading for anyone interested in Africa. Having fallen into disfavour with President Sékou Touré, Camara Laye suffered restrictions on his freedom for four years before deciding to emigrate. He died in Dakar in 1980. Shortly before his death he gave the following interview to Denis Herbstein.*

It took time to track down Camara Laye to his exile home in Dakar. He wasn't on the phone and nobody was sure of his precise address, except that it was in Amitié, the workers' quarter on the way out of town. Certainly, one of Africa's best-known writers was keeping the lowest of profiles in his adopted Senegal.

Then a journalist friend drew a circle on the map and said I would find him somewhere there. Just before the Avenue Bourguiba, left at the Bar le Coq Gaulois, and the first child kicking a football in the street directed me straight to house 3069, Rue 10, home of Camara Laye. *L'écrivain guinéen* is better known in the teeming *ruelles* around his house than in the elegant Plateau of Dakar's city centre.

Camara, calm and authoritative, says: 'I shall only go back home when Sékou Touré is no longer president. Even if he rules for a long time. . . .'

His extreme personal antipathy for Sékou Touré is to be compared with Victor Hugo's vow that he would not return from exile in the Channel Islands until Napoleon III was gone. The robust Hugo survived twenty years and returned

Camara Laye—Involuntary Exile

to see the Republic re-installed, even becoming a Deputy himself. Camara Laye at fifty-two is several years younger than Sékou Touré. But he is a sick man and unlikely to outlive him. He may never again see the Niger serpentining through Kouroussa, his birthplace in Upper Guinea.

He was born the eldest son of a goldsmith, and of the daughter of a goldsmith on the first day of 1928. Life in the family compound was steeped in the tradition of the Malinkes, heirs to the great Mali empire of medieval West Africa.

Soon other influences were brought to bear. Laye was an exceptionally bright child, sailing through his Koranic studies, primary school and eventually the Collège Poiret in Conakry. The college has since become the Lycée Technique, and most certainly in the new Guinea it is not just the name which has changed. But in the early 1940s, Camara and his bright contemporaries were being shaped into cosy Black Frenchmen and women. They learnt all about Napoleon and Vercingetorix, but the Guinean heroes of resistance to French conquest, Alpha Yaya and Samory Touré, whose campaigns were part of the recent folklore of the common people, were ignored. Black pupils knew the geography of France, department by department, but were hard put to learn about their own country. In language lessons; dictée, composition, elocution, recitation; Voltaire, Diderot, even Shakespeare. Little science and technical teaching. It was the censorship of deculturalization.

The promising lad from the hinterland won a scholarship to study motor mechanics in Paris. Arriving in France at the age of eighteen, a year after the end of the war, he stayed for another ten, so long that he wrote his nostalgic idyll, his *mémoire de jeunesse* namely *The African Child*. The Whites loved it, the Blacks thought it irrelevant. By the time it appeared in 1954, French Africa was in a ferment, with creative writing gripped by the fever of negritude. Yet here was a book which had nothing to say about what life was like for a Black under White domination. *Présence Africaine*, Paris mouthpiece of Black literature, reviewed it harshly: 'Has this young Guinean, of my own race, who it seems was a very lively boy, really seen nothing but a beautiful, peaceful and maternal Africa? Is it possible that Laye has not once witnessed a single minor extortion of the colonial authorities?'

Camara's second novel, *The Radiance of the King*, followed swiftly, and was actually dedicated to the High Commissioner for French West Africa. It did nothing, as Dorothy Blair says, to reconcile Camara with his Black detractors: 'This allegorical novel of quest and redemption seemed a gratuitous literary exercise to the exponents of commitment.'

Yet today, a generation later, the flame of militant negritude a mere after-glow, these two early works have become established and even revered on the African bookshelf. And on reflection, though they lacked the important ingredient of militant blackness, they did vaunt the traditions of old Africa, mourn their passing, much as Thomas Hardy mourned the past in his loving evocation of the English West Country.

After Guinea attained its independence, Camara was sent on diplomatic missions to Liberia and Ghana. A little later Touré appointed the first writer of the land to the directorship of the Ministry of Information's Study and Research Centre.

Camara's relations with Touré go back to childhood.

I knew Sékou Touré when I was six years old. He lived quite far away, but we knew the family. I also knew him in the early days round the time of independence. He was courteous with everyone, though it was the sincerity of the ambitious politician. Even when he was president, I used to attend meetings of the Conseil de Ministres [Cabinet] as an observer. I listened but did not talk. Sékou Touré did the talking and nobody contradicted him.

By 1960, Camara and a growing body of young intellectuals had fallen into disfavour with the president. It was early days, but already the high hopes of being able to live and create freely in the new Africa were being shattered. A regimen amounting almost to house arrest seriously restricted Camara's ability to work and travel. He stuck it out for four more years, during which time his father, Camara Comady, the dignified hero of *The African Child*, died. Then the author left.

I was not thrown out, but left because a writer cannot work when there is no freedom of expression. So in 1964 I played the *malade imaginaire* and said I was going to Paris for treatment. Instead I came to Dakar and found friends from Paris. I'm not saying the Senegal regime is better or worse than the Guinean. It is just easier here for me to create. There, I had no books to read, nobody to argue with. . . .

I started a book straight away on my arrival here. I had to purify (*désintoxiquer*) myself. I talked about nothing else. So I had to get Guinea out of my system . . .

That purification took the form of writing book number three, *A Dream of Africa*, which appeared first under the French title, *Dramouss*, in 1966. It is the Dream, or more correctly, the nightmare, which explains Camara's unyielding hatred for his former collaborator. European literary critics, looking back to his earlier work, thought little of the Dream, but we are concerned with its political statement.

In the book Camara still refuses to condemn colonialism. The hero, Fatoman, returns to his pre-independence Guinea from France and talks to an old friend:

> I don't think the moment has yet come in which to condemn or blame the colons. That moment will come when we are able to prove, through our abnegation, through our work, through our concrete achievements, that we are superior to them. . . . Certainly, there were some negative aspects, I admit, in colonialism. But when everything's taken into consideration, the influence of colonialization on this country was beneficial.

That sort of stuff is neither good for Fatoman nor for the man who writes it.

Back again in Conakry, Fatoman alias Camara attends one of those strident slogan-chanting Black nationalist gatherings which preceded the hand-over by the metropolis. He finds it altogether distasteful. Afterwards, he confides to a friend:

> Someone must say that though colonialism, vilified by that committee, was an evil thing in our country, the regime you are now introducing will be a catastrophe whose evil consequences will be felt for decades. Someone must speak out and say that a regime built on spilt blood through the activities of incendiaries of huts and houses is nothing but a regime of anarchy and dictatorship, a regime based on violence. . . .

The crucial chapter in the book is the 'dream' itself. It is an allegorical confrontation between the 'big brute', surely Sékou himself, and a White female figure called Dramouss.

The 'brute' Touré is Fatoman's (Camara's) jailer. 'Why are you throwing me into prison?' the hero/dreamer asks. Because 'you're getting on my nerves', he is told. They go on talking, and the dictator asks: 'Does goodness ever pay? . . . Now, you have a heart of incredible gentleness and sensitivity! . . . The heart of a mother for her offspring! . . . It's a disgrace to have such a good heart.

Goody-goodness ruins a man.' After which Fatoman is told that the next day will be his last.

But help is on the way in the form of the Black Snake, who springs Fatoman and advises him to 'remain good and keep your confidence in man. . . . If you had accepted the brute's point of view, I should not have saved you.' Snake anthropomorphizes into the ravishing Dramouss, and together they meet a Black Lion and Guinea is free.

Had Camara Laye been an exposé journalist, fleeing into exile with the inside story of how Guinea, the hope of progressive Africa, had so soon turned into a prison state, his cause might have been better served. But he is a novelist, and though the attack was direct and stern, it was still couched in the language of fiction. So that, unlike a journalist, he could be accused of hindsight in allowing Fatoman to predict before independence how things would go wrong after it.

Fifteen years later, Camara is even more sure that the book had to be written:

> I reproach Sékou Touré for destroying a society which is a thousand years old, and replacing it with the worst aspect of Russia and Hitler's Germany. Before him, we did not have concentration camps, dictatorships and torture . . . that's not my country, the most beautiful in Africa. I do not say that I want colonialism back. But I don't want Black people in its place who destroy our liberty.

The Dream is the only one of Camara's books to be banned in Guinea. Camara sent a copy to Sékou. 'He reads a lot, or somebody will have read it for him and it would have been understood to be about him.' Recently, after a gap of a dozen years, Camara published his fourth book *Le Maître de la Parole*—published by Collins, as *The Master of the Word*. (All his books, incidentally, have been translated into English by James Kirkup.) Camara digs into the Malinke past, telling their history through the *griot*, the soothsayers who, in countries where the written word is rare, are the archives, the guardians of the word, the conservers of tribal customs, history, legend, poetry and culture. Of course, the old Manding (Malinke is one of the languages spoken by the Manding peoples) empire covered most of modern Mali and Upper Guinea as well as a large chunk of Senegal. Camara cannot be thinking of restoring the old glories by redrawing geographical frontiers. But he objects strongly to the closed nature of Guinean society.

Camara Laye is a modest, self-effacing man, who likes to live among his family, avoiding the limelight. He is a conservative, albeit in the best sense of the word, intrigued by the mystical past, eschewing the 'isms' of Europe and the East, saying no more than 'If I were a politician I would leave people to themselves, like Houphouet-Boigny in the Ivory Coast.'

Few modern writers can be less well-suited to living in exile than Camara Laye. He is ill, with a kidney complaint and high blood pressure.

> I usually earn enough from writing to sustain my entourage, but when a domestic financial crisis occurs, I don't work well. I get blood pressure from the worry. . . . Had I continued to live in Kouroussa, I would have worked in tranquillity. The Malinke family is a collective. I have seven full and half brothers and sisters there. The sons and daughters would have worried about the house, while I spent my days writing.

The fact remains that, however painful his exile, this is where he has written his four books to date. He wrote about his childhood and early youth from abroad, and about the Malinke people from outside their territorial domain. Perhaps these things can only be done from exile, rather than from a molly-coddled existence in Upper Guinea. Could he have written these books at home in Guinea? 'Yes, but differently. The Guinea you see from France is idealized, nostalgic. The first exile was necessary to learn what Europeans could teach me. But this exile isn't voluntary. . . .'

Once more, I asked him: 'Will you ever see Guinea again?' He was not pessimistic. Sékou Touré's policy had indeed changed, and he had even embraced Houphouet-Boigny. 'But even if his policies ape those of Houphouet's, I will not return. I cannot say what it is, but I don't like the man.'

Camara chipped off a bit of kola nut, that mystical West African nibble, the bite that stimulates. Perhaps he knew more than the politicians of the West. Or he was mindful of the plight of that other renowned Guinean, Diallo Telli, persuaded to return home after being Secretary-General of the Organization of African Unity, only to die in one of Sékou's prisons.

'So I'll stay here.' A twinkle lit up his sad eyes. 'I've got my grandchildren to work for me.'

Searching for the Truth
WEI JINGSHENG

Wei Jingsheng, at sixteen a zealous Red Guard in Mao Zedong's Cultural Revolution, grew disillusioned with the ideology of Mao and with conditions in China, becoming one of the leading figures in the brief period of liberalization in 1978–9 known as the Peking Spring. An electrician by training, he edited Tansuo *('Explorations'), one of the best-known unofficial journals of the period. He was arrested in March 1979 and, after a short trial, sentenced to fifteen years' imprisonment. The following is an extract from his unpublished autobiography, written in prison, which appeared in* Index on Censorship *in 1981.*

I was sixteen when the Cultural Revolution broke out in 1966. Going by the normal system of schooling in China, that should have been the year I graduated from junior to senior middle school. But the Cultural Revolution threw everything into chaos, schooling included. Still, I think what our generation gained ideologically from the turmoil of the Cultural Revolution made up for what we lost by not being able to pursue our studies. During those troubled times people had to rid themselves of blind faith and prejudice, and continually scrutinize their way of thinking and looking at things. As a result, they had the chance to make a really objective analysis. Under ordinary circumstances that would have been out of the question.

My father was a low-level party bureaucrat, utterly devoted to Marxism-Leninism and the Thoughts of Mao Zedong. He did his utmost to instil Marxism-Leninism-Mao Zedong Thought into our minds, and encouraged us to read a number of political works, for example Liu Shaoqi's *On the Self-Cultivation of Communists* and Stalin's *Dialectical and*

Searching for the Truth

Historical Materialism. Even though I couldn't fully understand these books at the time, this kind of training turned me into a staunch believer in Marxism-Leninism-Mao Zedong Thought. In fact you could say that right up to the time when my happy illusions were shattered by what I saw in real life, I was a fanatical Maoist.

My mother also instilled a certain outlook on life in me, but in a different way from my father. While both she and my father were against us children reading novels, my mother often bought memoirs of the Communist Party's early revolutionary struggles and other books of that sort, and did her best to get us to read them. Judging from an argument I once overheard between my mother and father, my mother believed that we could only understand Marxism-Leninism-Mao Zedong Thought properly if we first learnt to distinguish emotionally between what to love and what to hate, and to commit ourselves emotionally to 'the people's standpoint'. She believed that if a young person didn't know *how* the people had suffered, he wouldn't begin to understand *why* they had suffered, and wouldn't know why a revolution had been needed. This upbringing my mother gave me had a decisive influence on the way my thinking later developed. Without it—without the revolutionary desire to 'make sacrifices for the suffering people's sake'—I might have ended up like other cadres' children, shrugging my shoulders at the sight of workers' and peasants' actual living conditions and talking glibly about 'the dark side of socialism'. I might have gone along with most other 'city dwellers' and 'children from families with good class backgrounds', complaining about 'loafers and scroungers' whenever I saw a dirty, foul-smelling beggar.

The bitter experience of the Cultural Revolution moulded an entire generation. When I joined the Red Guards along with a few dozen friends at the beginning of 1966, they were a fanatically Maoist organization. But at the same time they were an organization of people dissatisfied with reality. The latter quality was more important, for if they had simply been a group of Maoists there would have been no need for them to 'rebel'—to use the slogan of the time—in the way they did. Like me, most Red Guards were fed up with the lack of social equality in China. This gave them quite a spirit of self-sacrifice, which meant, in turn, that they formed an extremely strong—indeed, nearly invincible—fighting force.

So why, in the end, did they fail to destroy our social system, with all its inequalities? The reason is that they armed themselves mentally with the ideology of despotism. Take myself, for example. At that time I was, as I have said, an ardent Maoist. I saw that the fine things talked about in the works of Mao, Marx and Lenin had not been achieved in reality. And I saw that the leaders of our school evidently had no intention of achieving them. None of this seemed at all right to me. So when I heard Mao Zedong saying that class struggle still existed in the social stage of society, and when I heard him saying that class enemies had wormed their way into the ranks of the leadership, I saw that all the inequality and unhappiness of our society had been brought about by these class enemies who had wormed their way into the Party. Whereupon I threw myself wholeheartedly into the campaign to ferret out such creatures. I pictured them all to be like the actor who played Bukharin in the film *Lenin and the October Revolution*.

For all kinds of reasons the Red Guard movement quickly grew and spread throughout the country. We followed Mao Zedong's instructions, and went from place to place 'exchanging revolutionary experiences' and 'stirring up the fires of revolution'. The first thing we did when we got somewhere was to get in touch with local people we knew, people from all walks of life but mostly cadres of various ranks. We would find out from them about local cadres, and especially about 'the people in authority'. Then we would go down to schools, factories, mines and enterprises and try and get people to rebel. Once our initial enthusiasm had worn off, however, this sort of rebelliousness made us ask ourselves whether all 'those in authority' weren't equally bad. If this was indeed the case, it looked as though the entire country and Party had turned bad! Ideas like this didn't fit at all well with the ideas we had started out with.

When we got back from the provinces, we found an even more contradictory state of affairs in Peking. Elderly cadres that we knew and got on well with had been branded 'capitalist-roaders'. To us they didn't seem at all anti-Party or anti-socialist. Besides, they had been born into the 'exploited classes' and had joined the revolution at an early age. This kind of thing was none too easy for a sixteen-year-old to understand. Faced with predicaments of this sort, the Red Guards started to split up into factions. I decided that the situation was extremely complicated, and that the only way to explain things properly was to get more concrete information. So I set out with several close friends from school to carry out a social survey.

In the stations west of the city of Xian there were an extraordinary number of beggars. When I caught sight of beggars, I automatically handed over some of my food to them. Then the man opposite told me not to. 'They're probably bad class elements,' he said, 'former landlords or rich peasants. Anyway, they're lazy scroungers.' He spoke with a very persuasive air, so although I wasn't entirely convinced I took his advice. Even so, I sometimes saw small children begging, and I couldn't help feeling sorry for them or wanting to give them something to eat.

After entering the famous North-Western Corridor beyond Lanzhou, the train suddenly stopped at a tiny station. Evidently very few trains ever stopped there, and very few people ever got off. As soon as our express train came to a halt, it was surrounded by a crowd of beggars. I saw a woman with her face covered in ashes, and long hair hanging down loosely to conceal the upper part of her body. Apart from her hair, she had nothing that could be called clothing covering her body, only mud and ashes plastered all over it. . . .

During the next two days of the train journey, I couldn't put the scene on that anonymous little station out of my mind. Was the socialist system itself responsible? Or was it just the result of a rare case of bad leadership? I realized that it was nothing like enough to familiarize myself with conditions in the cities and the upper strata of society, and that I could only get a true picture of Chinese society by getting to know about life at the lowest levels, too.

With this aim in mind, I went with a friend of mine to see what life was like at the grassroots level in an army construction corps. Wherever we went we tried to make friends with people. We had an enthusiastic, straightforward way about us, and this made us a lot of friends among educated youths—young people sent down to the countryside after school or university—demobilized soldiers and people who had been stigmatized as 'rightists' in the late 1950s. We discovered that although they all had different aims in life, different histories and plights, they all had one basic thing in common: they were all dissatisfied. The educated youths and demobbed soldiers all felt they'd been cheated. An old rightist that we got to know told us straight out that when she first joined the Communist Party, she never thought that it could one day come under the control of the inhuman bunch of people then in charge. When we first heard her talking like this we were extremely shocked. But my friend and I always made a habit of listening patiently to each and every point of view; and with various little stories, including the story of her own life, she explained to us why she thought as she did with an authority and conviction that fascinated me.

Searching for the Truth 79

We soon became very close friends. She helped us to get to know a number of very poor people in the area, including an Uighur peasant who was chairman of a local poor peasants' association. After leaving his house I was struck by the feeling that we had gone back twenty years in time, and that what we had seen was the house of a poor peasant before 'liberation' such as you might read about in a novel. The only difference was that he was forever talking about 'revolution' and 'revisionism' as if to remind us that we were, after all, living in 1966 and not 1946. . . .

From about this time onwards, my state of mind became such that whenever I read descriptions in the newspaper of 'the superiority of socialism over capitalism', or heard someone pontificating on the subject, I would swear inwardly and dismiss it as so much bullshit. The capitalism I had read about in books may have been terrible, but I couldn't believe that there was anything worse about it than the things I had seen on my travels. I still reckoned that the things I'd seen were the result of people violating Mao Zedong's instructions, but I was beginning to wonder why Chairman Mao had always placed his trust in such people. . . .

After returning to Peking, I found that among those I got involved with there were people who proposed making a Marxist-Leninist re-evaluation of Mao Zedong Thought, and who said that 'before 1957 Chairman Mao was a great man, but after that he made mistakes'. Even today people don't always dare to say such things openly. At that time the effect of such remarks on most listeners was shattering. But for people like me they were like a light at the end of a tunnel. The fact that by 1967 Chairman Mao had already instructed Jiang Qing to turn heartlessly on us 'baby rebels' and arrest us was already undermining the esteem in which I had held the old man. Once people began alluding to his past record like this as well, I started wondering whether the Thoughts of Chairman Mao, too, did not have their 'problems'.

[By 1968 Wei Jingsheng found himself on the run from the authorities after opposing Mao's wife, Jiang Qing, and her political faction. He ended up in a village in Anhui Province.] I arrived in the countryside just in time for the 'campaign to purify class ranks' and various other political campaigns of the same sort, as well as big moves to build up Mao Zedong's personality cult. As these class struggles gradually took in more and more people, many of those who had previously stood firmly on the side of Maoism and the Communist Party found themselves lumped in with those to be struggled against and overthrown. I started wondering whether class struggle really was as serious as these campaigns made it out to be. The way I saw it, after liberation in 1949 those who had been landlords and rich peasants before then no longer enjoyed any privileged economic status. If there was any common interest that still served to bind them into a single class, it was their new-found status as the oppressed rather than the oppressors. As for those oppressing them, most workers and peasants had neither the power nor the need to do so. Anyhow, going by the Marxist view that 'economic status determines class', weren't former landlords and rich peasants now members of the same class as ordinary workers and peasants? Cadres, on the other hand, had far more power and far higher economic and political status than workers and peasants. So didn't they constitute a class of their own?

From a commonsense point of view, I had always been aware that these two classes—cadres on the one hand, workers and peasants on the other—were as different as oil and water. But it was only after making a theoretical appraisal of the problem on the basis of the Marxist method of class analysis that I understood it clearly. I had the exhilarating feeling of having just woken up from a dream, even though I was still conscious of being enveloped in darkness. I was struck with full force by the fact that I could no longer trust to any of my old ideas or theories, and that everything would have to be reappraised and re-examined. Henceforth I took advantage of the quiet of the countryside to read through the classic works of Marx, Engels, Lenin and Stalin. The ones I found most convincing were those by Marx and Engels. It seemed to me that their theories were far more scientific than the others. There was only one work of Lenin's that I liked, and that was *State and Revolution*, particularly the part about proletarian democracy.

During this period the lingering after-effects of the Great Leap Forward and 'communist wind' of the late 1950s that were still visible in the countryside left a particularly deep impression on me. I often heard peasants talking about the Great Leap Forward, which they referred to as though it had been an apocalypse. When they discussed it they had the air of people conscious of their good fortune in escaping from a disaster. I couldn't help being extremely interested, and pressed people for details. Gradually I realized that the 'three years of natural disasters', as they were known, had been the result not of nature but of mistaken government policies. For example, the peasants said that as a result of the 'communist wind' of 1959–60 people had been too weak from malnutrition to gather in a fine rice harvest, and quite a few of them had simply starved to death watching the 'wind' blow the rice-shoots flat in the paddies. In some cases whole villages had left their crops unharvested in this way. Once I went with a relative to visit a village a mile or so from where I was living, and we passed through a deserted village. None of the houses had roofs—only their mud walls were left standing. I thought the village must have been amalgamated with another one in line with the policies of the Great Leap Forward, so I asked my relative why the mud walls hadn't been knocked down and the land ploughed up.

'People still own these houses,' he told me. 'The walls can't be knocked down without the owners' consent.'

The houses were clearly derelict, so I couldn't see how anyone was living in them.

'No, of course no one's living in them. Everyone in this village starved to death or vanished at the time of the "communist wind". Up till now no one's ever come back here, which is why the land's been divided among the nearest production teams. But they used to say that one day someone or other might turn up again, so the houses were left untouched. I don't suppose there's much chance of anyone coming back now, after all these years!'

We were just passing by the edge of the village, and the bright sun on the green weeds pushing up between the mud walls—a sharp contrast to the neat paddy fields around us—lent a further air of desolation to the place. The sight of those weeds conjured up a vision of the barter in children's flesh that I had heard about on my visits in the neighbourhood. I had a vivid picture in my mind of the agony on the faces of men and women driven to eating the flesh of other families' children, children taken in exchange for their own. . . . Who had driven them to this cannibalism? I knew then that the man responsible, a bloody tyrant unparalleled in Chinese history, was none other than Mao Zedong. I understood at last why the peasants detested 'communism'. They didn't want to give people their own children to eat; they didn't want to be driven to such distraction that they beat their own friends to death for food. They wanted to go on living. These were more substantial grounds for feeling as they did than any ideology.

During the year or more that I spent in the countryside, I saw for myself how Mao Zedong's theory of class struggle was put into practice in real life. Mao Zedong relied on this method of dividing the people into different—and imaginary—interest groups as a way of concealing from them where their true interest lay, and of getting them to slaughter one another for the sake of objectives that not only went against but also damaged their own interests. Only thus could he secure the support of the hundreds of millions of people that he tricked and oppressed. Only thus could he hide his tyrannical features and masquerade as the people's leader.

Translated by Peter Harris

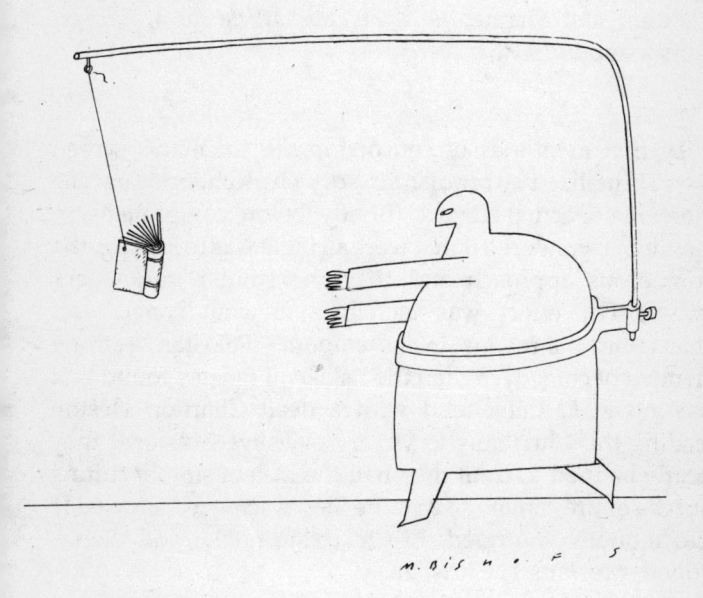

Casualties of Censorship
SALMAN RUSHDIE

Born in Bombay, Salman Rushdie is a highly acclaimed novelist and winner of the Booker Prize in 1981. The author of Midnight's Children *and* Shame, *he wrote this article for* Index on Censorship *in 1983.*

My first memories of censorship are cinematic: screen kisses brutalized by prudish scissors which chopped out the moments of actual contact. (Briefly, before comprehension dawned, I wondered if that were all there was to kissing, the languorous approach and then the sudden turkey-jerk away.) The effect was usually somewhat comic, and censorship still retains, in contemporary Pakistan, a strong element of comedy. When the Pakistani censors found that the movie *El Cid* ended with a dead Charlton Heston leading the Christians to victory over live Muslims, they nearly banned it, until they had the idea of simply cutting out the entire climax, so that the film as screened showed El Cid mortally wounded, El Cid dying nobly, and then it ended. Muslims 1, Christians 0.

The comedy is sometimes black. The burning of the film *Kissa Kursi Ka* ('Tale of a Chair') during Mrs Gandhi's Emergency rule in India is notorious; and, in Pakistan, a reader's letter to the *Pakistan Times*, in support of the decision to ban the film *Gandhi* because of its unflattering portrayal of M. A. Jinnah, criticized certain 'liberal elements' for having dared to suggest that the film should be released so that Pakistanis could make up their own minds about it. If they were less broad-minded, the letter-writer suggested, these persons would be better citizens of Pakistan.

My first direct encounter with censorship took place in 1968, when I was twenty-one, fresh out of Cambridge and full of the radical fervour of that famous year. I returned to Karachi where a small magazine commissioned me to write a piece about my impressions on returning home. I remember very little about this piece (mercifully, memory is a censor, too), except that it was not at all political. It tended, I think, to linger melodramatically on images of dying horses with flies settling on their eyeballs. You can imagine the sort of thing. Anyway, I submitted my piece, and a couple of weeks later was told by the magazine's editor that the Press Council, the national censors, had banned it completely. Now it so happened that I had an uncle on the Press Council, and in a very unradical, string-pulling mood I thought I'd just go and see him and everything would be sorted out. He looked tired when I confronted him. 'Publication,' he said immovably, 'would not be in your best interests.' I never found out why.

Next I persuaded Karachi TV to let me produce and act in Edward Albee's *The Zoo Story*, which they liked because it was forty-five minutes long, had a cast of two and required only a park bench for a set. I then had to go through a series of astonishing censorship conferences. The character I played had a long monologue in which he described his landlady's dog's repeated attacks on him. In an attempt to befriend the dog, he bought it half a dozen hamburgers. The dog refused the hamburgers and attacked him again. 'I was offended,' I was supposed to say. 'It was six perfectly good hamburgers with not enough pork in them to make it disgusting.' 'Pork,' a TV executive told me solemnly, 'is a four-letter word.' He had said the same thing about 'sex', and 'homosexual', but this time I argued back. The text, I pleaded, was saying the right thing about pork. Pork, in Albee's view, made hamburgers so disgusting that even dogs refused them. This was superb anti-pork propaganda. It must stay. 'You don't see,' the executive told me, wearing the same tired expression as my uncle had, 'the word "pork" may not be spoken on Pakistan television.' And that was that. I also had to cut the line about God being a coloured queen who wears a kimono and plucks his eyebrows.

The point I'm making is not that censorship is a source of amusement, which it usually isn't, but that—in Pakistan, at any rate—it is everywhere, inescapable, permitting no appeal. In India the authorities control the media that matter—radio and television—and allow some leeway to the press, comforted by their knowledge of the country's low literacy level. In Pakistan they go further. They control not only the press, but the journalists, too. At the recent conference of the Non-Aligned Movement in New Delhi the Pakistan press corps was notable for its fearfulness. Each member was worried that one of the other guys might inform on him when they returned—for drinking, for instance, or consorting too closely with Hindus, or performing other unpatriotic acts. Indian journalists were deeply depressed by the sight of their opposite numbers behaving like scared rabbits one moment and quislings the next.

What are the effects of total censorship? Obviously, the absence of information and the presence of lies. During Mr Bhutto's campaign of genocide in Baluchistan, the news media remained silent. Officially, Baluchistan was at peace. Those who died, died unofficial deaths. It must have comforted them to know that the state's truth declared them all to be alive. Another example: you will not find the involvement of Pakistan's military rulers with the booming heroin industry much discussed in the country's news media. Yet this is what underlies General Zia's concern for the lot of the Afghan refugees. It is Afghan free enterprise that runs the Pakistan heroin business, and they have had the good sense to make sure that they make the army rich as well as themselves. How fortunate that the Qur'an does not mention anything about the ethics of heroin pushing.

But the worst, most insidious effect of censorship is that, in the end, it can deaden the imagination of the people. Where there is no debate, it is hard to go on remembering, every day, that there is a suppressed side to every argument. It becomes almost impossible to conceive of what the suppressed things might be. It becomes easy to think that what has been suppressed was valueless anyway, or so dangerous that it needed to be suppressed. And then the victory of the censor is total. The anti-*Gandhi* letter-writer who recommended narrow-mindedness as a national virtue is one such casualty of censorship; he loves Big Brother—or *Burra Bhai*, perhaps.

It seems, now, that General Zia's days are numbered. I do not believe that the present disturbances are the end, but they are the beginning of the end, because they show that the people have lost their fear of his brutal regime, and if the people cease to be afraid, he is done for. But Pakistan's big test will come after the end of dictatorship, after the restoration of civilian rule and free elections, whenever that is, in one year or two or five; because if leaders do not then emerge who are willing to lift censorship, to permit dissent, to believe and to demonstrate that opposition is the bedrock of democracy, then, I am afraid, the last chance will have been lost. For the moment, however, one can hope.

Manuscripts Banned and Destroyed
PRAMOEDYA ANANTA TOER

Pramoedya Ananta Toer was imprisoned in the Buru Island detention camp in Indonesia from 1965 to 1980. While there, he wrote two historical novels which were published in Jakarta shortly after his release, but then banned by the authorities, who arrested both the author and his publisher and ordered 10,000 copies of the books to be burned. While Pramoedya was released after interrogation, the publisher, Joesoef Ishak, spent several months in police custody. Pramoedya wrote the following article for Index on Censorship *in 1981.*

The imposition of bans on literary works in colonial and totalitarian countries is but a reflection of the jealousy of those in power.

In 1935, I saw an official of the colonial power confiscate books written by my own father. One morning, a few days later, hundreds of beautifully printed books—the works of someone living in our town—floated on waters swirling under a bridge. He was afraid of having to confront those in power, and preferred to surrender his writings to the river. This took place in colonial days, in a small town, and it was not reported in the press.

I have known about bans since I was young, during colonial times. That such things should be inflicted after independence on my own writings and those of many others is something that needs to be discussed.

The first time manuscripts of mine were destroyed was in 1947, by Dutch marines. Earlier, the Dutch colonial army confiscated diaries I had been keeping since 1938. It was a time of revolution in Indonesia, a time when lives were at stake and no one bemoaned the loss or destruction of manuscripts. Fortunately, a few of these writings had been published a couple of months earlier. But most of what I lost then has not been recovered to this day. They were notes about the armed struggle in east Jakarta, written in the form of a novel—documentation of the Indonesian revolution.

It was in 1960 that a work of mine was banned for the first time, *The Overseas Chinese in Indonesia*. I heard about the ban while I was abroad, and when I returned home, I was summoned for an explanation by Supreme War Command. [Indonesia was then in a 'state of siege and war'—Tr.]. My interrogator was Sudharmono, a graduate of the Military Law Academy, and I was not allowed to go home but kept in a military prison in Jakarta. Another interrogator who said he was a graduate from Al Azhar, Egypt, accused me of 'selling the Indonesian state to the Chinese People's Republic' with that book. There was no arrest warrant. This can probably be described as a case of 'kidnapping'. Two months passed at the military prison, then I was taken to Sudharmono again. The charge: I wanted to escape. As additional punishment, I was transferred to Cipinang Prison. I was put into a block in the front of the prison. Most of the men in this block, secured with double doors, were prisoners who had gone mad. It was also the block for convicted prisoners who were being punished for misdemeanours.

During this period of detention among these mad people, I felt the need to make notes about their behaviour. These notes were subsequently vandalized in 1965, though some had already been published in the *Lentera* column of *Bintang Timur*.

I was released from prison in a ceremony held on Supreme War Command premises, together with rebels from Sulawesi and Sumatra. The next day, my name was mentioned in press reports together with the names of these rebels. After my release, I was held under house arrest, then under town arrest.

The time I spent behind double doors in Cipinang Prison is among the most bitter of all my experiences. There was a lavatory in my tiny cell which led directly to a drain under the floor. The walls of the cell were covered with flies from the lavatory. The sounds coming from the cells of the people who had gone mad were quite unbearable.

My family was never told anything about me during this period of detention. My wife was in the final stages of pregnancy, and it was in this condition that she had to go round, looking everywhere for me; she finally tracked me down at the military prison. A few weeks later, she gave birth. By announcing our baby's birth in the press she was able to inform people about my arrest. On the basis of this, Radio Australia broadcast a report that the Indonesian Government had for the first time taken action against a Communist. Yet, right up to the end of this period of detention, lasting almost a year, there was no sign that a trial would take place. I was thus convicted without trial.

That was my first experience of detention after Indonesia became independent, and under a government of my own nation.

After my release, the political situation in Indonesia grew increasingly critical. Western democracy, liberal democracy, proved to be unsuited to a nation whose character had been formed during more than three centuries of colonial rule. In an attempt to discover a form of its own, Indonesia chose guided democracy. This led to conflicts with the major powers, who regard the world as being in a state of immutable conflict between East and West. Indonesia's internal conflicts entered the area of international conflict.

I am no étatist, yet seeing the crisis of those days, I considered it a luxury, even something immoral, to remain indifferent about national affairs and succumb to self-indulgence. This was true particularly of literature. If under those conditions I started polemics by calling for an end to persistent self-indulgence in literature and appealing for a sense of commitment to Indonesia's affairs, this was certainly not over-acting. They were open polemics and, as is the case with all polemics, the aim was the search for truth.

This was the start of a period of more than fourteen years in detention. In 1966, I read from a torn piece of newspaper reaching us in Tangerang Prison that all my works had been banned; this ban had come from a department with no authority to impose prohibitions. I was not able to understand from the explanation given why it was considered necessary to ban my works.

During my more than fourteen years of detention, I was slandered on innumerable occasions in writing and in print, without being able to defend myself. I have had no opportunity to this day to prove that all these allegations are false.

In all former colonies, democracy and with it the freedom to create has not been lawfully inherited from colonialism. It must be nurtured by each and every individual in all the formerly colonized nations.

The fact that to this very day, all my works are still banned is but a small illustration of the condition of a formerly colonized nation, a social-historical product that must look strange to those nations that have enjoyed western democracy for seven or eight generations. This is quite illogical. And it was precisely for the sake of creative freedom that I had to pay so dearly, with the loss of my own freedom for more than fourteen years plus the loss of rights and possessions for which, to this very day, no one is willing to accept responsibility.

A few basic points need to be stressed: that Indonesia, only a few decades old, is still searching for the most appropriate form for itself, that democracy was not a lawful legacy from colonialism, and that each and every artist is challenged to create his own conditions for creative freedom; so, until such time as the law is capable of protecting personal property and understands too that creations are the personal property of their creators, it is up to each writer and artist to safeguard his or her own works. Each possession faces the risk of being damaged or lost, of being stolen, seized or destroyed. All this depends on the cultural level of a nation and the laws that have been brought into existence for it.

During my period of detention in Buru, I was able to acquire a typewriter. Although I then started writing with what energy still remained, I had foreseen the possibility that my writings would be seized, and this is indeed what happened.

With General Sumitro's visit to Buru in 1973, the circumstances of a few friends including myself underwent some changes. He promised us the earliest possible release and said that 'while waiting for this time to come', we should start practising our professions again. As detainees, we had become immune to promises as well as to threats. The fact that our 'earliest possible' release took seven years coming only shows just how cheap our freedom had become. But precisely because of this, it was a period of trial for me in finding ways to safeguard my own works. Freedom is the crown of life: how true that is! Even under conditions of freedom, one's rights and personal possessions, even one's freedom, can be seized; without freedom, it's even worse. I was in the last batch of prisoners to be returned to Java. Just before this group of prisoners left, there came an official instruction from the authorities: all books and writings must be examined. I knew perfectly well that this instruction had been issued especially for me. And indeed, just before I left Buru, those in command refused to return my papers to me. Yet again, my possessions were being seized, even though I had given the authorities a copy of every single thing I had written. Precisely because of this,

I quite deliberately used the word 'seizure', premeditated seizure.

Only two months after I returned to my family in Jakarta, a naval captain, Heri Herriono, came to seize all the manuscripts I had saved, and he hasn't yet returned any of them to me. Thank goodness, Indonesia has saved some of them with the generous help of some people.

Since we were in Buru, Hasjim Rachmad and I had agreed that we would publish my Buru works. Give me the honour of publishing them, he said. And I agreed. Just an unwritten agreement, without proof, without witnesses, but in the back of our minds we realized: publishing something is an expression of democracy. And the condition of publishing as a whole gives an idea of the state of democracy as a whole.

After returning to Jakarta, we learnt that several publishers had had the intention of publishing some of my pre-Buru and Buru works but never had the opportunity to do so. Thus, when the publishing company, Hasta Mitra, consisting of Hasjim Rachmad, Joesoef Ishak and me, published *Bumi Manusia* in August 1980, this was done as a contribution towards the development of democracy in Indonesia. And, however small this may be as a contribution, it represents too a contribution towards humanity throughout the world. Each literary work published is a bridge for mutual understanding between fellow human beings and between nations.

At the end of May 1981, Indonesia's Attorney-General banned two Buru works. This came as no surprise to me, having seen how those in power had confiscated the books of my own father, how a book of mine had been banned in 1960, having seen the acts of vandalism against my works in 1965–6 as well as the seizure of my manuscripts at the end of 1979 and then again in 1980. But those in power are not always the ones who control justice and truth although it is true that they can control the courts.

At the very least, some progress has been achieved in Indonesia in the way the ban was imposed, which is quite encouraging. In previous cases, bans were imposed simply by being written down on a sheet of paper on the instructions of superiors, then being typed out by reliable secretaries. This time it was not so simple. Before the ban was imposed, people in several provincial capitals and in other smaller places had to be mobilized to discredit me personally and to discredit my works. This process lasted for no less than two months.

Tiny though this may be, I regard it as a sign of progress for democracy, not democracy inherited as the lawful legacy from colonialism but democracy resulting from our own efforts. Another step in the right direction can be added to this first one if we include the statements, published as well as unpublished, before and after the ban, disagreeing with the bans, and also positive responses including some from individuals in positions of power, written as well as verbal.

These two tiny signs of progress give reason to hope that in Indonesia, my own motherland, publication of my works will encounter fewer and fewer obstacles, maybe tomorrow or the day after.

Translated by Carmel Budiardjo

From the Darkness
KIM CHI-HA

Kim Chi-Ha, South Korea's most famous poet, wrote 'From the Darkness' in prison in Seoul in 1974. Originally sentenced to death, he was released in 1975, then rearrested and again released. His prison poems were printed in Index on Censorship *in 1975.*

From the Darkness

From the darkness yonder
Someone is calling me
A pair of glaring eyes lurking in the darkness
The blood-red darkness
Of rusty prison bars.
Silence beckons me
And clogged, halting breath.

On a rainy day of grey lowering clouds
Faltering through the calls
Of pigeons cooing in the eaves
It keeps calling and calling me
A tattered blood-stained shirt
Hanging from the window sill
That red soul which thrashed through endless cellar-nights
The congealed cry of a body racked and torn
Beckoning me
Beckoning me.
The silence yonder is calling me
Calling on my blood
To refuse
To refuse all lies.

From the darkness yonder
On a rainy day of grey lowering clouds
From that darkness of blood-red bodies
A pair of glaring eyes.

Translated by J. de Yepes

My Ten Uncensorable Years, or How Liver-sausage Lost its Political Implications
STANISLAW BARAŃCZAK

Stanislaw Barańczak is a well-known Polish poet and critic who, with several other prominent writers, was responsible for starting Zapis, *the unofficial literary quarterly launched in 1977. It printed the banned works of Polish authors and became one of the most popular of the many uncensored publications circulating in Poland. He has been lecturing at Harvard University in the USA since 1981, when he wrote 'My Ten Uncensorable Years' for* Index on Censorship.

One day in August 1971 I was sitting in the editorial office of a state publishing house somewhere in Poland, arguing about the term 'liver-sausage'. This appeared in one of my poems in a volume which was just about to go to press. The editor, who was responsible for the 'ideological profile' of the books put out by this publishing house, suggested that I should censor the poem myself.

'Liver-sausage'—she explained to me gently and patiently—'is the cheapest pork-butcher's product. The poem gives the impression that the average Pole often eats liver-sausage, and this in turn may be understood as an assertion that there is a meat shortage in Poland.'

'But there *is* a shortage of meat!' I countered naïvely, forgetting to add that the poem was in any case concerned with other matters than exposing the problems of the meat market.

The editor glanced at the young author indulgently.

'Surely we understand each other, dear colleague. That poem won't get through in any case.'

'The liver-sausage stays in.'

Rather than allow myself to be persuaded to replace liver-sausage with something like salami or steak, I withdrew the entire poem from the volume.

For me, this whole story of the liver-sausage embodied the symbolic beginning of my writing career in the 1970s— years which, whether I liked it or not, were dominated by censorship problems: coping with the censorship, by-passing the censorship and, finally, open confrontation with the censorship.

This decade had an equally symbolic conclusion. On a certain evening in June 1980 I found myself sitting in the police station at the main Poznan railway station, arguing about a book by a Polish poet, which they proposed to confiscate. A quarter of an hour earlier, security service agents had detained me on the platform as I alighted from the train that had brought me from Warsaw. I had experienced such encounters several times before. As a member of a Workers' Defence Committee (KOR) and a contributor to the independent publications, I was being watched by the police; and a watchdog from the security force suspected, not without good reason, that every journey of mine to Warsaw was associated with the delivery of some copies of the most recent publications to appear 'outside the censorship' i.e. independently and unofficially. After being searched a couple of times, always in the same railway police station, I ceased to act as a distributor, this role being taken over by someone less well known to the police.

On this occasion, however, at the end of June 1980, I had succumbed to a bibliophile's passion. A volume of poems by a certain Polish poet had been published by the independent publishing house NOWA, the most attractive product to appear so far from the uncensored publishers.

My Ten Uncensorable Years

Quite simply, I could not resist taking this elegantly produced little book back with me to my home town. For safety's sake, I put it not into my bag, which was usually searched, but under my shirt. But my precautions were of no avail. The policeman who was patting me with his hands felt an untypical growth on my body and, with a triumphant cry, extracted the book from under my shirt. With equal triumph the Polish poet's work was confiscated as 'evidence in the matter of disseminating illegal publications'. I have the form recording the confiscation to this day.

The author of the confiscated volume was Czeslaw Milosz. The security officers who searched me naturally could not foresee that some weeks later Milosz would be awarded the Nobel Prize for literature, and that this writer, whose works were banned by the censor and published only by independent publishers who were harassed by searches and arrests, would suddenly become a source of our national pride. Nor could the security officers be expected to foresee that in August, even before the Nobel award, the striking workers in the Gdansk shipyards would include among their demands an end to the harassment of independent publications and checks on the arbitrary lawless pressures exerted by the censorship.

So when on that June evening I left the police station, with the record of the search in my pocket instead of Milosz's book, I had no intimation that something was drawing to a close, that a particular era was ending. On the contrary, I felt dejected at the thought that ahead of us all—writers, publishers, printers—lay long years of exhausting guerrilla warfare with those whose occupation and vocation in life appeared to be the suppression of every manifestation of free thought and free speech.

I do not mean to say that today—after all the triumphs of Solidarity, after the rapid expansion of the network of uncensored publications, after the passing of a new law on censorship—an ideal situation has been achieved in Poland as regards free speech and publication. On the contrary, the struggle continues, censorship and the political police are still there, and the new censorship law is imperfect and unsatisfactory. Like everyone, I realize this and have not succumbed to euphoria. None the less I do consider that since August 1980 a qualitative change has taken place in the relations between the principle of free speech and the censorship. This change has arisen from the fact that a conviction about the need to defend the truth (truth in the spheres of information and news, of history and of culture) has become the shared possession of the whole of Polish society.

This enables one to look back at the seventies as a period which is in a certain sense ended. When I try to answer the question—what did that period give me personally?—I can find only one word for it: freedom. For me, the whole decade involved the gradual realization of a simple fact, that the only responsibility of a writer is to present what he has to say about the world in a way that is complete and artistically pure. If he is to carry out that responsibility, he should be free of censorship of all kinds, whether external or internal. There is no price too great for a writer to pay for such freedom. It is even worth paying the price involved in descending into the literary underground, being absent from the official market, having limited contact with one's readers. I do not say this because this kind of strategy has ended with success in the particular case of Poland. Even had there been no victory, and we had been facing another decade of uphill struggle, I should still think the price worth paying.

I came to this conviction by two parallel routes. During the seventies I worked not only as a writer, but also as an editor of literary journals. This has enabled me to look at the question of literary freedom from two viewpoints—separate viewpoints, because in countries like Poland the interests of the editor or publisher do not always coincide with those of the writer.

In any case, the authorities' tactics consist in stirring up dissension between those two interests. I gained experience of this in the early years of the seventies, when I was running the literary section in a certain 'socio-cultural' monthly in the provinces. I took up my post in conditions of relative cultural liveliness and considerable freedom of expression. The first months of Gierek's rule—not unlike Gomulka's October in 1956—brought with them a fairly extensive 'thaw'. This made itself felt even on our provincial journal, which was then experiencing its golden age and was regarded as one of the most interesting publications in Poland. The idyll was, however, short-lived. From 1972 onwards, the chief editor began to call me in more and more frequently for talks. During these he would try to impress on me the necessity of providing what he called a 'consistent line' for the lively disorder which passed for policy in my section. Just what this policy was to be was not clear. On the other hand, it was clear that certain writers, critics and even translators whom I had, on the editor's behalf, invited to work with us in the past were becoming gradually less and less welcome. It was also clear, and made increasingly explicit, that I was expected, when preparing the copy for the printer, to check not only for literary accuracy but also for ideological conformity.

When it became clear that I was supposed to play the same sort of role as that editor who—at more or less the same time—had cut the ideologically suspect term 'liver-sausage' from my poem, I decided to leave my editorial post. The moment of decision followed a particular minor incident. I had specially commissioned a translation of a piece of prose by the Soviet writer Bulat Okudjawa; but I was told to return it to the translator because, in the meantime, Okudjawa had apparently fallen into disfavour in the Soviet Union. I found this explanation so absurd that I immediately handed in my resignation.

At this important moment in my literary life, I at last

understood the nature of the phenomenon which had been taking shape for some time, but which I had hitherto tried to disregard. The cultural policy of the seventies — dominated by the grim figure of its party boss Jerzy Lukaszewicz—was based on the simple principle of 'divide and rule'. In a normal and freely developing literary milieu, the publisher or the editor of a journal are in principle the writer's allies. Both sides are equally concerned with reaching the reader. In a country in which literary life is shackled by censorship, the situation can vary. It may happen, of course, that a publisher has a certain independence and remains the writer's ally. They work together to try and push the work through the sieve of censorship. This was how it was in Poland during the successive periods of 'thaw'. On the other hand, once a publisher has the remnants of his independence removed, a situation can be reached in which the interests of the publisher and the writer diverge. The publisher is interested not so much in actually publishing the book as in preserving his good reputation in the eyes of authority and thus holding on to his position. This was the objective of the seventies. At a certain moment, publishers and editors were made responsible for the ideological or political content of the works published by them. By this single move, the directors of our culture ensured that publishers ceased to be the writer's ally and became the censor's assistant. From that moment there was no longer any place among the publishers for anyone who was merely interested in making literature of artistic merit available to the reader. (Here I am thinking of the state publishing houses and publications, not of the Catholic publishers, who formed an exception to the rule because they retained a certain measure of independence.) Even if someone cherished the illusion that he was continuing to perform such an independent function, the pressure of everyday concessions and compromises was sooner or later bound to make him move to the other side of the barricade.

This is why the appearance a couple of years later of the first texts published and circulated 'outside the censorship' was treated from the outset as a tremendous and salutary opportunity for literature. Naturally not everyone felt this. Even among those writers who had suffered severely in their tussles with censorship and the official publishers, some could be heard to say that evasion of censorship could expose the whole of Polish literature to disaster, to the emergence in Poland of a 'Czechoslovak solution', to drastic reprisals and to the withdrawal of the remnants of freedom through police terror. These reactions were hardly surprising. Those who expressed similar views could remember not only the example of Czechoslovakia but also the recent pogrom against Polish culture in March 1968 and the somewhat earlier trials of writers and distributors of exile publications. Thus uncensored publications simply constituted a precedent whose consequences—which might also ultimately include penal sanctions—no one was in a position to predict. Past analogies, however, inclined one to draw pessimistic conclusions.

In spite of this, a group of writers came together to found *Zapis* ('The Record')—the first uncensored literary journal in history with a completely overt editorial staff. Shortly afterwards a second publication of this type was started, entitled *Puls* ('Pulse'). The independent publishing house NOWA also embarked on a lively programme; much of its output consists of contemporary works by writers in Poland.

For me, as an editor of and a contributor to these papers and publications, one thing has been important in the whole enterprise. At last I can, as an editor, once again be the ally of the writer. I can work on a paper which, while it does not pay me a monthly salary, gives me something much more important—a feeling that I am making a contribution to the shaping of contemporary literary activity.

At the same time, I have a feeling of honest participation in the literature itself. The creation of an uncensored publishing and circulation network has made it possible for me, as for many other writers, to reconcile two hitherto incompatible desires: the desire for freedom from censorship and the wish for one's writing to reach the reader. Up till then, only one of these two desires could be realized. One possibility was to have one's works published, printed and available in the bookshops—but then one had to accept the interference of the external censorship and one's own self-censorship. The alternative was to write entirely free of censorship—but to write for one's desk drawer or for the exile press, whose publications reach the readers in Poland in very small numbers. The birth of publications operating outside the censorship has almost entirely done away with these alternatives. I say 'almost' because the way in which they operate in society is after all not quite the same as that of the official literary circuit. It is true that NOWA is publishing editions of increasing size; that the technical level and the graphical presentation have improved, that there is a growing number of independent publications and that the distribution network continues to improve. But despite all this, every writer realizes that this is not the same as publishing a 'normal' book, one which is later discussed in 'normal' literary journals and on sale in 'normal' bookshops.

As I write this, however, I immediately ask myself whether I am not somehow wrong. What exactly is 'normal'? Is it not the case that the rise of uncensored publications has restored some saving normality to us—the normality of literature reaching the reader at first hand, without having to squeeze itself through the censor's filters and sieves?

This is an important question, because solving the

problem of what exactly is 'normal' involves taking one or another view of the future of literary activity in Poland. For instance, in view of the undoubted recent easing of censorship and the curbing of its activities under the new law, should the publication of papers and books outside the censorship cease? So far as I am concerned, I would never agree to this. And to my knowledge, such a decision is also rejected by the independent publishers and the overwhelming majority of writers connected with them. So long as the censorship exists, the independent network operating outside the censorship must also exist. We have become too accustomed to complete freedom in writing and publishing: it has become an essential condition of our existence, not a luxury, but the air which we breathe. It is, of course, very pleasant to return after several years to the pages of the official literary periodicals, or to publish a book in a state publishing house. But I am certain of one thing: so long as the censorship lasts, I shall be involved in continual conflicts with it. This being the case, I shall continue to need an outlet where I can publish without heeding the censorship.

When I look back at the last decade, it seems to me that as well as the freedom to write I also gained something else—that priceless value which in our absurd part of the world constitutes normality. One must, however, realize that in literary life freedom is not synonymous with normality, though an essential condition of it. In my particular case, these two values did not become accessible to me simultaneously.

My first liberation as a writer from both external and internal censorship was accomplished, in my view, in the long poem 'Artificial Breathing'. This was written in the years 1971–4 in the full awareness that the work was unpublishable: it was in fact first of all circulated for several years in manuscript as samizdat, then published abroad. This was poetry that was free, though not yet normal. In this first major work, written without the constraint of censorship, I wanted to say too many things at once, to expound my view of the world in too much of a hurry. Today, in consequence, I am not satisfied with all sections of the poems: some of them seem to me to be superficial and journalistic in style.

On the other hand, I hope that in my next collection (*I Know it Isn't Right*) and particularly in the latest (*Triptych of Concrete, Exhaustion and Snow*) I succeeded in writing normally, that is to say—not against the censorship but putting it out of my mind entirely. This was the stage at which freedom enabled me to attain normality. It was of course linked with the rapid growth of independent publications which occurred during those years. Writing without censorship had become so widespread by then that there would have been no point in making a special virtue of it. In the same way, there would be no point in constantly stressing the fact that people prefer to breathe clean air and not poison gas. In such a situation, literature, having said what it had to say on subjects hitherto forbidden, could return to normality, i.e., to its normal responsibilities—to Conrad's 'dispensation of justice to the visible world' in all its complexity and complications.

To return to the symbolic frame of my uncensorable decade, which was the subject of the early part of this essay. The struggle with the censorship in countries like Poland is waged not so much to defend the possibility of expressing opinions not accepted by the authorities, as to defend normality against absurdity. This struggle is waged not only so that it should be possible in Poland to read works by Poland's greatest living poet without fear of having the book confiscated by the police. It is also being waged so that one should be able to use the term 'liver-sausage' in a poem without provoking a search for political implications. The point is that a word should be a word and a value a value;

My Ten Uncensorable Years

the psychological well-being of society should not be deformed by concealment, by ambiguous implications, or by uncontrolled outbursts. In short, we should be able to live, write, read and think as free and normal people.

Translated by Sheila Patterson

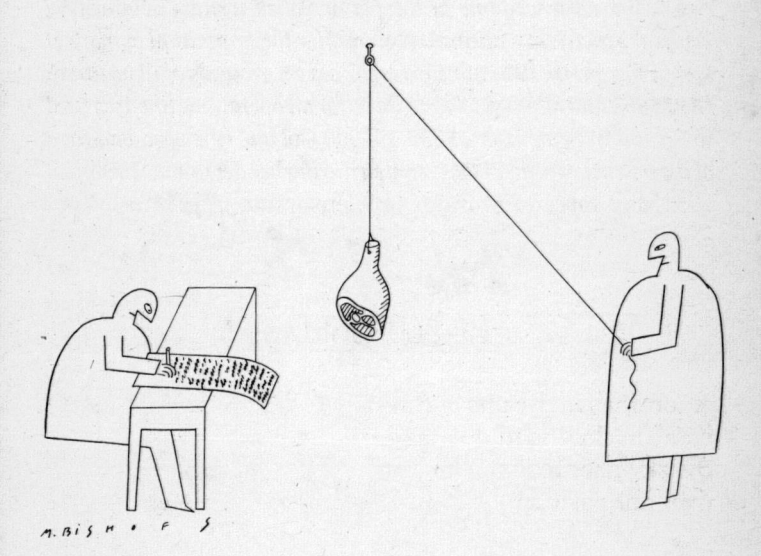

19—500 Goldap
ANKA KOWALSKA

Anka Kowalska was one of the many Polish writers detained by General Jaruzelski's military regime after the imposition of martial law in December 1981. She was released on grounds of ill health in May 1982 and allowed to go to Paris for an operation. She returned to Poland in September 1983. '19–500 Goldap' (the postal address of the detention centre) was written during her detention, in March 1982, and appeared in Index on Censorship *in 1983.*

19–500 Goldap

A forest as in dreams of forests
snow in childhood dreams
the sky rises blue
over our pastoral

Those concussed are at last taken to hospital
those lamed during the last transport can now walk
and that one who's been lying facing the wall these last three days
is just a hysteric
isn't the Children's Home looking after her child

Behind the door of a tiny room marked 'Chambermaid'
they are today questioning Wroclaw
the police from Gorzów are here
the car with a Warsaw registration is gone
they are probably drinking in Suwalki

Several women had letters from home
which said that seven weeks
ago
the husband was arrested
granny was well
father had a heart attack but wasn't too bad

A Red Cross commission arrived
'Have you any problems? Are you ladies hungry?
Are you in touch with home?'
'They threatened executions they threatened Siberia'
'But now you are all right? We see you have baths'
'Our families took a long time to find us'
'Well, it's wartime post—and now?'
'Now I've received a letter two months old'
'That's excellent'
'There's a woman here with tubercular kidneys'
'Make a note of this, we must somehow'
'Security are forcing her to collaborate'
'That, madam, is not our business
We are the Red Cross'

The coaches are gone
the guests are leaving
the women's place is full of palms and rhododendrons
in a forest in a dream
horses seem to step in a sleigh carnival dance

It's the sentries' hooves scraping the glassy frost

Translated by Adam Czerniawski

The Last Time I Went to Press
VICTOR NEKRASOV

Victor Nekrasov, until his fall from favour in 1972, was a popular Soviet writer whose war novel, In the Trenches of Stalingrad, *won the Stalin Prize for Literature in 1946. He was expelled from the Writers Union for defending Solzhenitsyn and other dissidents, quickly becoming a 'non-person'. His long entry in the official Soviet Encyclopedia was deleted and he was no longer allowed to publish. He left the Soviet Union in 1974 and now lives in Paris.*

Sitting one evening over a drink in one of the homes outside Moscow where writers go to work, I asked a pleasant, elderly Lithuanian writer how he used to be published in his own little Lithuania in the days before it became the fourteenth or fifteenth republic among equals.

He gave a slight smile:

'How did I use to be published? Well, I took my manuscript to a publisher.'

'Naturally.'

'The publisher weighed it in his hand and asked me what it was about. I answered that it was about such and such. . . .'

'And then?'

'A bottle of wine or a little vodka. And in a day or two I'd get the galley-proofs.'

'And the book?'

'In ten or twelve days. Sometimes even sooner. . . .'

I sighed. My own book had been lying at the publisher's getting on for two years. And that was regarded as normal.

But this was a long time ago, when they were still publishing me. Later they stopped.

What's it like when they stop publishing you?

On the basis of my own experience I can say that they do it very gallantly.

It began a long time ago, three years ago, perhaps even more. I went to the editorial office of a respectable Moscow journal which had been publishing my writings for twenty years, said that I had a suggestion for a manuscript, and outlined the content. At that time I was still held in high esteem; I had not been expelled from the Party. They were obliging and affable with me. Drew up a contract and gave me a 60 per cent advance. I shook hands all round, thanked them and went home. Some time later I returned to the office with my manuscript. They read it, made one or two comments, nothing of importance, I would say, and sent it for typesetting. A day or two later I received the proofs, checked them through, and. . . .

Here I shall permit myself a small digression. This all took place in March 1972. But in January of that year two gentlemen had turned up at my flat, presented the appropriate warrant and expressed a polite interest in whether there were any books in my library prohibited by law. By the end of their visit it had been ascertained that there were such books: *The First Circle*, *Doctor Zhivago*, and the *Memoirs* of Nadezhda Mandelshtam; and I was obliged to part with them.

That had been in January. And in March. . . . To cut a long story short, I came back to the editorial office with my corrected proofs, whereupon they took me aside and informed me in a whisper: 'The type has been broken up . . . but don't let on to anyone that you know. . . .' With an innocent air I dropped in to see the editor-in-chief, a likeable man who thought very well of me.

'You know,' he said, without batting an eyelid, 'I've read your manuscript over again, and it seems to me that to make it even better it would be worth your while to add one or two things. In your own style. One or two arguments. How does the idea strike you?'

'All right,' I said, pretending that the arguments he had suggested would indeed improve the book. 'All right,' I said, and I went off to the Crimea to add something in my own style.

The summer went by. I returned to Moscow and went to see the editor. He was as obliging and affable as ever.

'How did your holiday go? And your work?'

'Splendidly.'

I handed him the additional reflections in 'my own style'. The next day this same editor—undoubtedly a good man, who had lost none of his friendly regard for me—after saying how highly he rated my talent, my eye, and so forth, suggested (in order to improve the work still further, for he had no doubt that it would) that I make a couple of alterations here and here, and another one here too. . . .

We never met again. I simply submitted a request to his deputy for the manuscript to be returned to me and the rest of the money paid. My goodness, how overjoyed they all were. True, they did, out of politeness, express a little indignation: 'It's always the same, we delay and delay and as a result we lose our authors . . .', but they could hardly conceal their joy at having finally parted company with such a difficult writer.

I was more than a little downcast, but my friends came to me and said: 'Don't fret, old man, go and take the manuscript to this or that journal instead. The chief editor there is an old front-liner, I believe he was even at Stalingrad, he's sure to love you.'

I muttered something about the character of the journal, but they laughed me down and so, my manuscript tucked under my arm, I set off to see the front-liner from Stalingrad.

I was welcomed with open arms. The following morning they read the manuscript, signed a contract and paid me 60 per cent, and I went home rubbing my hands. They had promised to publish it in a particular issue.

A month passed, and another. Autumn came, bringing with it, as well as the rains, certain changes in my fortunes. I was summoned to the Party committee of the Writers Union, where they told me that, after reviewing the course of my life and my literary work, they had reached the conclusion that I could not remain within the ranks of the Party. Well, I began going to interviews with Party investigators and attending various Party commissions, but that is another story and I shall save it for some other time.

The people at the journal I had visited that spring were very distressed. 'You understand the position we're in. We'd like to publish you but we can't. . . . If all this business with you ends happily we'll publish you straightaway, in a flash. After all, it's a fine piece of writing. . . .'

But the ending was not happy. I was expelled from the Party.

Just before leaving to go abroad, I called in at the editorial office. Despite the very different character of the journal, nobody there was pleased. Indeed, they were grieved—it was a fine piece of writing. And I didn't have to write and ask them: they paid me the remaining 40 per cent, bade me farewell, and wished me: 'Well, what can we wish you? Success. . . .' We parted friends.

Incidentally, when I took my leave of top Party leaders in Kiev who had called me in for an interview, good manners prompted me to wish them success—the senior of the two success in his public career, and his assistant, who was also a writer, success in the literary sphere. Both pressed their hands to their heart, but they did not wish me anything.

Well, that is all. I have brought the manuscript with me. I am curious to know what a third editorial office will say to me. Perhaps, as happened to my old friend, they will weigh it in their hands, ask what it's about and send it to the compositor. And ten or twelve days later. . . . But that was in tiny Lithuania. A long time ago. And paper was cheaper.

Translated by Hilary Sternberg

The Censor
IVAN KRAUS

Ivan Kraus, a witty Czech author and puppeteer, was one of the artists who started the first Black Theatre of Prague in the 1960s. He emigrated after the Soviet invasion in the summer of 1968 and has made his home in West Germany. 'The Censor' comes from his collection of short satirical pieces and appeared in Index on Censorship *in 1976.*

The Censor

The Censor is seated on a stool (or possibly two stools).
The Dancer enters.
At a sign from the Censor she begins to dance.
Censor: More slowly, please.
The Dancer continues to dance.
The Censor stops her.
Censor: Hold it! Show me that last movement again.
The Dancer does so.
The Censor shakes his head.
Censor: No, no, no. Leave that out.
The Dancer resumes her dance.
Censor: No. Not that. Omit it.
The Dancer dances.
Censor: That's not allowed.
The Dancer again resumes dancing.
Censor: Omit!
(after a while)
   Omit!
(after a while)
   Leave out!
(after a while)

And that!
The Dancer no longer dances, she is merely walking about the stage.
Censor: What's this? Call that a dance? Why aren't you dancing?
The Dancer shrugs her shoulders helplessly.
Censor: Don't do that!
The Curtain starts to come down.
Censor: Just a moment!
The Curtain stops.
Censor: I won't stand for any innuendo. Gently, now . . . that's better . . . gently . . . very, very slowly . . .

The End

Translated by George Theiner

A Cup of Coffee with My Interrogator
LUDVÍK VACULÍK

Ludvík Vaculík, a banned Czech journalist and novelist, spent many years in the 1970s bringing out the Edice Petlice *('Padlock Publications') samizdat series of banned Czech authors, to which he contributed his own regular* feuilletons. *One of these—based on his experience of police interrogations following the birth of the Charter 77 human rights movement—was 'A Cup of Coffee with My Interrogator', published in* Index on Censorship *in 1977.*

Unless you have been through it yourself, you wouldn't believe how difficult it is to avoid replying to polite questions. Not only does it go against the grain not to reply, because of one's good upbringing, but it is also difficult to keep up because it is hard on the ears. A beginner finds it next to impossible. Worst of all, it doesn't make for good relations between the parties concerned, the rift thus created being often insurmountable. Which is what I mean to write about.

Undeterred by his lack of success, Lieut.-Colonel Noga began anew each morning: 'Would you please get your papers ready, Blanička.' His secretary, Blanka, took out a clean sheet of paper, carbons and flimsies, put them in her typewriter and, fingers poised above the keyboard, turned her face towards her boss. He hesitated while he thought out his question, then he asked me, 'Would you care for a cup of coffee?' I decided to accept the coffee.

Lieut.-Colonel Noga is a smallish man, well-built, dark of skin and hair. Originally a factory worker, his behaviour and speech indicate that he has spent many years in a different environment. His Czech is correct, but there is something about his pronunciation which hints at another Slav language. This wretched detail made me, willy nilly, adopt a kind of coquetry one tends to employ when dealing with fellow-countrymen.*

'All right, Mr Vaculík, you insist that your conduct isn't in breach of the law. Let's just suppose you're right,' he was fond of saying. Then he would add, 'Well then, why don't you tell me about it.'

'I'm sorry, Lieut.-Colonel,' I would reply, 'but I really don't feel I want to go over all that again.'

'You don't feel you want to? What kind of talk is that? Why don't you say exactly what you mean—after all, this is *your* protocol: "I refuse to testify!" '

Mrs Blanka looked up at me, I nodded shamefacedly, and she typed the words.

'When will you return my things to me?' I asked, pointing at the two suitcases standing beside his desk.

'Don't confuse the issue. Next question—take this down, Blanička: What is your opinion . . . of the way the western press . . . is misusing the whole affair . . . for its slanderous campaign against Czechoslovakia?'

I dictated my reply: 'I will answer this question as soon as I have had an opportunity to read what the western press has to say on the subject.'

'You so-and-so!' he rebuked me in mock anger, left the room and came back with a whole pile of foreign newspapers, which he slammed on the desk in front of me.

I requested Mrs Blanka to record: 'When I say I want to read foreign newspapers, I mean when I can buy them at a news stand.'

In the course of that week of interrogations I was able

---

*Like Vaculík himself, the interrogator comes from Moravia.

to put any number of such impertinences into my statement. No one objected.

One evening there were just the two of us, as Mrs Blanka went home at four. He sat down on her stool, turned the roller in the typewriter, and said, 'Here we've been at it all day and we've got just seven pages. Not very much, is it?'

'There isn't going to be any more,' I replied.

'Oh really? There is, you know.'

'All right, tell me something about nocturnal interrogation.'

He cast an alarmed eye at his watch. 'Half-past seven already! But that still doesn't make it night.'

'Either have me put in a cell or send me home. But first of all, take me to the toilet.'

'Oh no, we don't lock up witnesses. I will take you to the toilet, though. Have you got some paper?'

I hadn't any, and so he picked up two clean sheets, crumpled them obligingly and handed them to me. Then he waited outside the toilet. Seeing that we had been at it all day, those two sheets were scarcely sufficient.

Already on the second day it was clear to me that it was more of a siege than an interrogation. Once I had repeated my initial refusal, there was really nothing else for us to do. My Lieut.-Colonel was in the habit of leaving the room for long periods at a time. As for Mrs Blanka, she found me a dreadful bore. On the first few days she tried to win me over.

'Why don't you want to testify? No one is punished for expressing his opinions. You ought to hear how we complain about the office canteen!'

'Yes, but just imagine that one day the canteen manager is given powers to have you all locked up.'

'Oh, but that's absurd!'

'Isn't it. And then imagine it happening on a nationwide scale.'

She shook her head at this, smiling like one who is amazed at a child's foolishness. Then she said, 'Here the law is being respected, you know. For instance, the prisoners have a right to exercise, and look!' She beckoned me to the window.

She was speaking the gospel truth: down there in the courtyard, in deep, concrete pens, I could see the prisoners, dressed in brown, circling round, talking and laughing.

Every lunchtime Lieut.-Colonel Noga escorted me to a little waiting-room, furnished something like a club. There I would be given frankfurters. On my way I would encounter Václav Havel or Professor Patočka. Most of all, however, I bumped into Dr Jiří Hájek. A friendly young woman always asked us, in Slovak: 'Would you like a coffee after lunch?' A pleasant interlude.

'Today,' said Dr Hájek, 'I gave them a little lecture on why I thought the demand for Czechoslovakia's neutrality in August '68 was a mistake.'

I was surprised. 'Do you mean to say you were *against* neutrality?'

It was his turn to be surprised. 'So you also thought I advocated it?'

'Everyone thinks so,' I told him. 'Why, only yesterday they were saying as much on TV.'

'But it simply isn't true,' he said, and with all the patience of thin men who wear thick-lensed glasses, gave me a little lecture on why he thought the demand for Czechoslovakia's neutrality in August '68 had been a mistake.

Once Mrs Blanka had to leave us in order to have her flu injection, and the Lieut.-Colonel and I were left on our own. He paced up and down the office, his hands behind his back, and I knew he was about to say something.

'Now the girl's gone, I'll tell you something man to man.' I pricked up my ears. 'Modern medicine, that is, psychology and sexology . . .' a few more paces, 'are agreed in the view . . .' a few more paces, 'that where a man and a woman are concerned . . .' he stopped abruptly in front of me, 'anything goes.'

Mm, I thought cautiously. He gave me a smile and wagged a good-humoured finger at me. 'But you, you really deserve a thrashing.'

In these circumstances it is best to keep quiet and try to divine what the man is leading up to. I am afraid I failed to divine it.

He took two red apples from his briefcase and gave me one. I asked what sort it was, and he told me, but I have since forgotten it. What interested me was that the apples came from a tree that was only five years old and he had several kilos of them. And I was touched by his giving me one. So I told him what sort of apple trees I had out at Dobřichovice. 'If I have to come back here again,' I said, 'and if I'm allowed to go there on Sunday, I'll bring you some.'

'Why shouldn't you be allowed?' he asked.

Next day, instead of my briefcase I took a big shopping bag and filled it with everything I had heard a detainee ought to have.

'You've brought a different bag,' he said at once.

'That's right. Today I either leave here a free citizen who doesn't get hauled in every day, or you must allocate me a cell.'

He was taken aback. 'Why, has anything happened?'

'I'll tell you what's happened. Here you are politeness itself, and out there in the street brutalities are taking place.'

'I've heard something—'

'And so you can keep your politeness. And let me tell you something I haven't told you before: when they brought me in for the first time, Martinovsky told me I was under arrest, took away my house keys and said they were going to carry out a search. What can you tell me about that?'

'He said you were under arrest and took your keys?'
'That's right.'
'Well, I wouldn't consider that proper.'
'In that case, give me back my things.'

He sat down behind his desk, saying nothing and with an annoyed expression on his face. Mrs Blanka looked shattered. Then Lieut.-Colonel Noga said: 'Do you want coffee?'

'No, I don't,' I replied.

I no longer remember what we put down in my statement that morning. At noon he wanted to take me to lunch as usual. I refused. He inclined his head to one side dispiritedly and said, 'You are really angry, aren't you? But why are you angry with me? Have I not shown good faith?'

'No, you haven't. If you had, you would at least have returned my manuscript.'

His brow furrowed, he dashed out of the office, returned and threw a file in black cardboard covers on the desk. 'There! But now you will go to lunch?'

A crisp winter afternoon was advancing behind the bars from the White Mountain towards the darkness. My Lieut.-Colonel was standing by the window, his hands behind his back. From the courtyard came the sound of women's voices as female prisoners took their exercise.

'Look, Mr Vaculík,' he said with a smile I could not see from where I was sitting, 'I know you'll put all this into one of your articles. . . .'

'I expect so, if I'm given half a chance.'

He was silent for a while. Then:

'And you'll call it: "A Cup of Coffee with the Interrogator".'

I almost fell off the chair. It was no use—they knew everything.

The next day—it was a Friday—I had a pleasant

surprise: they returned fifty-three volumes of 'Padlock Publications'. I couldn't get them all into the suitcase. Lieut.-Colonel Noga brought me a box, himself packed the books into it, tied it up and even made a little loop for me to carry it by.

'There, I've wrapped them up for you so nicely that I almost regret it.'

On Sunday I went to Dobřichovice for the apples. And that evening, when I was beginning to think they wouldn't come and they did arrive with yet another summons, I prepared a paper bag with samples of four different sorts of apple. . . .

But on Monday, what a change! Well, so be it.

'Sit down,' he said coldly. Mrs Blanka had her typewriter all ready and she, too, looked as if she didn't know me. My Lieut.-Colonel thought for a bit and then said, 'Have you changed your attitude over the weekend?'

I haven't, I thought, but *you* have. 'No,' I said out loud.

'And do you know how the workers are reacting?'

'Yes, I do.'

'What if I were to put you in a car and take you to a factory and ask you to defend what you have written in front of the workers?'

'First of all I'd ask them if they had actually read what we have written.'

He got up and hurried out of the room.

Now he's going to find me some workers, I thought.

He returned to his desk.

'Want some coffee?' he asked.

I didn't feel like coffee. 'Yes,' I replied.

Again he dashed out, maybe just to order the coffee, but he was gone for a suspiciously long time. Everything suddenly seemed suspicious to me, including the fact that they had returned those books. Mrs Blanka sat in silence. From the courtyard came the sound of men's voices, occasional laughter. I listened hard, trying to discern if Jiří

Lederer was perhaps laughing down there now, or František Pavlíček or Václav Havel.*

No, I said to myself in sudden resolve. Chickenshit!

He came back, sat down at his desk and snapped at me: 'Do you know Jiří Lederer?'

'Yes.'

'Did you give him your articles to send abroad?'

'Look, Lieutenant-Colonel, let's be clear about this: you've been on about these articles of mine for two years now. Are they criminal? If not, it can't be a criminal offence to send them abroad either. I'm telling you this off the record. For the protocol, all I'm willing to say is: I refuse to testify.'

Lunch. Jiří Hájek was already there when I arrived. We ate our frankfurters. 'Would you like a coffee?'

Jiří Hájek thanked her and said, 'You're looking after us so well that we'll grow fat in here and then won't be able to get out between the bars, and you'll say it's all our own fault.'

The girl laughed. 'Oh dear me, no!'

In the lift, as the Lieut.-Colonel escorted me towards the exit, I still debated with myself about those apples in the paper bag. But I stuck to my resolve: No. Chickenshit! Perhaps it was hard of me, but it was just.

Prague, 20 January 1977
(Copy to Lieut.-Colonel Noga)

Translated by George Theiner

---

*Jiří Lederer, a journalist, and the playwrights František Pavlíček and Václav Havel (together with stage director Ota Ornest) were arrested in January. Havel, as well as Dr Jiří Hájek and the late Professor Jan Patočka, acted as a spokesman for the Charter. Professor Patočka died on 13 March following police interrogation, while Dr Hájek, who was Minister of Foreign Affairs at the time of the 1968 invasion, is under constant surveillance.

Slit Lips
SAMIH AL-QASIM

Samih al-Qasim is a well-known Palestinian poet who lives in Haifa. When he published his collection Waiting For the Thunderbird, *he omitted to send it to the military censor for approval; as a result, he says, 'I was confiscated and my book was arrested.' His detention evoked strong international protest and he was released. His poem, 'Slit Lips', was published in* Index on Censorship *in 1983.*

Slit Lips

I would have liked to tell you
The story of a nightingale that died
I would have liked to tell you
The story . . .
                Had they not slit my lips.

Translated by Abdullah al-Udhari

Dr Azudi, the Professional
REZA BARAHENI

Reza Baraheni, an Iranian writer and academic, was imprisoned and tortured by the Shah's Savak secret police in 1973. He then spent some years in the USA before returning to Tehran after the fall of the Shah. His present whereabouts is unknown, but he is thought to be in hiding. 'Doctor Azudi', one of his prison poems, was published in Index on Censorship *in 1976.*

Doctor Azudi, the Professional

Azudi is just like
Genghis Khan   when he walks
he walks on a pile of fresh corpses

the Khan did not clean his teeth either
the Khan also belched   the Khan
did not take off his boots either   Azudi
has shattered the mouths of twenty poets today

Azudi wears a tie   something
Genghis Khan never did
only this splendid detail reveals the prodigious march of history

Eyewitness to Death
MUZAFFER ERDOST

Ilhan Erdost, a left-wing Turkish publisher, was detained for possessing banned books in Ankara on 5 November 1980. Two days later he was killed by the soldiers who were escorting him from an interrogation. His elder brother, Muzaffer, a publisher and writer, was with him when he died and he wrote an account of their treatment by the military authorities. This was published in Index on Censorship *in 1981.*

That evening we were kept at the same place of detention, the Security Directorate. Next morning, 7 November, we were again brought before the Martial Law Authorities. We waited there until late afternoon. At five-thirty, after working hours, the policeman who had escorted us was called to the magistrate's office, returning a little later with the news that we were to be put under military detention. To our question as to which article of the law had been given for our offence, he replied that no article had been mentioned and that the reason for our detention was 'having banned publications'. Since possession of banned books is not an offence, we had expected to be released. There was no reason for our being taken into custody.

My uncle was waiting outside, having come to take us to the prison in his car. My wife was with him. Under the supervision of the policeman we drove there, getting out of the car at a place close to the prison. Since I had been imprisoned several times before, my wife was used to such things and had always been calm. Yet this time, when we got out of the car, we saw that she was crying.

Ilhan laughed and said, 'Rana, this is the first time we see you crying at the prison gate.'

My wife said, 'Ilhan, I feel there's something different this time.'

While we waited outside, the procedures for our committal were completed. We were assigned to Block C. Having been in this prison twice before—once for fifteen days and the other time two years—I was able to tell Ilhan that Block C was not so bad, as it afforded a view. It was Ilhan's first imprisonment.

Before we entered, they asked what our political views were. We said 'Left', and they wrote this on our detention papers. We were first taken to a small room in Block A where photographs are taken and records are kept. There were three others already there and two more were brought in after us. They lined us up on the stairs, our backs to the wall. Before they shaved our hair and moustaches they took our photographs, from the front and from the side. Then they shaved us and again took photographs.

Each of us was given a card to fill in. The spaces where our appearance was to be described were filled by a soldier, who kept us standing at attention as he did so. The soldiers insulted us, beat us with their truncheons, kicking and hitting the ones they considered to be behaving improperly. Ilhan and I were twice hit on the hands while we stood in line. They then separated us from the other detainees.

The soldier who had written down the details of our appearance telephoned someone to say that there were two detained people to be taken to Block C, asking for a car and for a non-commissioned officer who would take charge. A little later an NCO came in and asked 'which ones'. They pointed to me and my brother. The NCO was followed by a soldier, and two other soldiers stood by the door. We were standing at attention, our backs to the wall next to the door. The soldier who had come in with the NCO asked what our crime was. We said 'having banned publications'. He asked 'That is?' At first I didn't understand what he meant—he was asking whether we were politically on the left or the right. We said 'Left'. Then they took us out.

In the corridor they searched our belongings again, removing our toothbrushes and tubes of toothpaste. The NCO said to one of the soldiers, 'Take them, you can give them to someone else.' Turning to us, he said, 'You even poisoned ten-year-old kids. The prisons are full of people like you.' As we climbed into the van, they started kicking us and hitting us with their truncheons.

The prison van had two compartments, with a door with a bolt separating them. Four soldiers with truncheons in hand got in and before the van started they came to the prisoners' compartment where we were and ordered us to stand up. I and my brother stood at attention and they started to hit our hands with truncheons, two hitting me and the other two my brother. They were lashing out without pity, with all their strength. After a while I started to yell. My brother said nothing. They were kicking, striking and hitting us with truncheons. I saw my brother stumble and fall on the floor. He was having difficulty getting up, but the soldiers went on kicking and beating him. Six years ago my brother had a disc operation. 'His backbone is broken, don't beat him, beat me,' I pleaded. Nobody listened. Because of the slaps and blows on my face I wasn't able to see my brother properly. It was dark and there were no lights in the van. As we drove off I could see the lights outside through the small barred windows. I again saw my brother being beaten, trying to stand up. I think this beating took half an hour. The van stopped. They opened the back door and took us out still beating and kicking us. As we were walking towards the prison, we were told to stop. All of them, including the NCO, started to beat us again. We were beaten for five more minutes. It was unbearable, and we asked the NCO to stop it. He said, 'You should have thought of this before.' Taking his words as encouragement, the soldiers began to beat us more violently. I saw my brother fall again. He couldn't get up. They were on him, kicking, hitting, striking. With difficulty he got up. They told us to stand at attention even though our feet could no longer carry us. Our hands were swollen like logs. We weren't able to keep them at our sides. The NCO shouted, 'Keep your hands at your sides, you have only your testicles to worry about.' When the soldiers heard this they started to beat us again. Some time later the NCO told the soldiers to stop. When we arrived at the door, they started beating us again. We heard some orders being given. My brother fell once more. Then he got up with great difficulty and we stood at attention by the door, two soldiers on each side. Others were yelling from behind, 'Attention, put your hands by your sides.' Three trusties came running, several prisoners took me by the arm, several others my brother. For a moment our eyes met. His face was covered with blood, his eyes were bloodshot. We looked at each other and said nothing.

My brother took two more steps and said, 'I feel sick, I am going to vomit.' He was about to fall. The prisoners took him by the arm and laid him down on a bed, taking me inside. They took his shirt off. I saw my brother as they brought him to the bed beside me. My brother was there, kneeling on one leg, his head lolling, his mouth open.

I called, 'Ilhan, Ilhan.' There was no reply. 'Ilhan, Ilhan,' I called again. They told me he would be all right. He must have fainted, I thought. They laid him on the bed just beside me. There was a medical student called 'doctor' by the other prisoners. He tried artificial respiration.

'My brother is dead,' I said.

'No, no, nothing is wrong, his pulse is a little weak, we are trying to help him,' they answered.

Fifteen minutes later an NCO came, and asked for a doctor. After another fifteen minutes, a medical orderly came and asked for an ambulance. They took my brother out on a stretcher. Very tall, his mouth open, eyes half closed. I wanted to kiss him, but the other prisoners didn't let me. My brother was gone, he had died just beside me.

I felt damp with sweat all over. There was a cold wind. I was being taken to some other place. I was shivering and was about to fall. They wrapped my jacket over my head to stop me from shivering. We walked some 400 metres and came to the officers' casino. The NCO who had brought us to the prison was watching television. 'Mr Muzaffer, why didn't you tell us that your brother had a heart problem?' My brother had no problem with his heart. I was conscious enough to know that he had died from brain damage. I was silent all this time.

I drank some water. Then they took me to a room in Section G. The officials gave me an injection to put me to sleep. I slept a little. I was constantly talking to my brother. Soldiers on guard were watching me through the window. After many hours, it was finally morning.

That day (8 November) they told me to get ready. Two prisoners helped me to dress. My arms and hands were swollen. They couldn't fit my wrists into the handcuffs. The soldiers told me that they had to put on the handcuffs, and they put them on without locking them. Then I was taken to Block A in a small van. I must point out several facts. When we were taken to the prison in the bigger van we were not handcuffed. Yet there are instructions that every detained or arrested person should be handcuffed even when being taken from one building to another. They knew that we would be able to protect ourselves, mainly our heads, with the handcuffs. Secondly, when they took me to the prosecutor's office in the small prison van, I saw that this would take at least ten persons, but it was not high enough for one to stand up, nor was it wide enough for four persons to beat two others. If we had been taken to the prison in such a van, they could not have beaten us in the way they had done.

In the prosecutor's office, they recorded my statement, they put down all I had to say. The next day I made a new statement. I added certain points. I was told by the prosecutor that there were only three soldiers on duty in that van and that he was searching for the fourth soldier who was in the truck even though not on duty. Later he found out who this soldier was. The NCO told the prosecutor that we were only beaten in the van and that he knew nothing about the incident. The soldiers stated that they had never beaten us. On Monday, I was again taken to the prosecutor's office to identify some soldiers. I asked if my family had been informed of the incident. I was told that this was the responsibility of the Martial Law Command. They asked me through whom my family could be informed if the Martial Law Command had not already done so. I told them that Halit Celenk, our lawyer and family friend could be informed. Four days had passed since the death of my brother and nobody outside the prison knew about it. On Monday afternoon Halit Celenk was told and he informed the family. The Martial Law authorities gave an official explanation. The next day Halit Celenk visited me. He told me that he had applied for my release and the military prosecutor had agreed. After the evening roll-call I learned that I was to be released. I passed the places I had earlier passed with my brother. They brought me to the entrance, where my uncle was waiting. 'We went in together,' I said, 'but I've come back alone.'

Stop the Lie
SIPHO SEPAMLA

Sipho Sepamla, a leading South African poet whose collection of verse, The Soweto I Love, *was published in London after being banned in South Africa, is one of those writers who bear out André Brink's statement: 'Black writing has become one of the most important factors pushing for change in South Africa.' His poem, 'Stop the Lie' first appeared in the Johannesburg magazine* Staffrider *in April 1981 and was reprinted in* Index on Censorship *later that year.*

Stop the Lie

I've always wished
you would listen
not to the cries of despair
but the substance of words
read from the frown of my brow
because those twists of flesh
carry the shouting of a new voice

   I want you to stop the lie
   don't tell me how much you feed the poor
   because you made hunger
   when you dropped those of my blood into the hole of gold

   I want you to stop the lie
   don't tell me of the schools you've built
   because you made ignorance
   by creating an education only for my kind

Stop the Lie

I want you to stop the lie
don't tell me of numbers of clinics and hospitals operating

because you made disease
when you paid pittance for all my labour

I've always wished
you would see me
not by the exaggerations of the eye
but in the shape of God's creation
seen in the fullness of my being
because I stand complete on earth
like men in the whole universe.

A Writer's Freedom
NADINE GORDIMER

Nadine Gordimer, the leading South African novelist, delivered the following paper at a conference on South African writing held by the Indian Teachers Association in Durban in September 1975. It was printed in Index on Censorship *the following year.*

What is a writer's freedom?

To me it is his right to maintain and publish to the world a deep, intense, private view of the situation in which he finds his society. If he is to work as well as he can, he must take, and be granted, freedom from the public conformity of political interpretation, morals and tastes.

Living when we do, where we do, as we do, 'freedom' leaps to mind as a political concept exclusively—and when people think of freedom for writers they visualize at once the great mound of burnt, banned and proscribed books our civilization has piled up; a pyre to which our own country has added and is adding its contribution. The right to be left alone to write what one pleases is not an academic issue to those of us who live and work in South Africa. The private view always has been and always will be a source of fear and anger to proponents of a way of life, such as the White man's in South Africa, that does not bear looking at except in the light of a special self-justificatory doctrine.

All that the writer can do, as a writer, is to go on writing the *truth as he sees it*. That is what I mean by his 'private view' of events, whether they be the great public ones of wars and revolutions, or the individual and intimate ones of daily, personal life.

Bannings and banishments are terrible known hazards a writer must face, and many have faced, if the writer belongs where freedom of expression, among other freedoms, is withheld, but sometimes creativity is frozen rather than destroyed. A Thomas Mann survives exile to write a *Dr Faustus*; a Pasternak smuggles *Dr Zhivago* out of a ten-year silence; a Solzhenitsyn emerges with his terrible world intact in the map of *The Gulag Archipelago*; nearer our home continent: a Chinua Achebe, writing from America, does not trim his prose to please a Nigerian regime under which he cannot live. You can burn the books, but the integrity of creative artists is not incarnate on paper any more than on canvas—it survives so long as the artist himself cannot be persuaded, cajoled or frightened into betraying it.

All this, hard though it is to live, is the part of the writer's fight for freedom the *world* finds easiest to understand.

There is another threat to that freedom, in any country where political freedom is withheld. It is a more insidious one, and one of which fewer people will be aware. It's a threat which comes from the very strength of the writer's opposition to repression of political freedom. That other, paradoxically wider, composite freedom—the freedom of his private view of life, may be threatened by the very awareness of *what is expected of him*. And often what is expected of him is conformity to an orthodoxy of opposition.

There will be those who regard him as their mouthpiece; people whose ideals, as a human being, he shares, and whose cause, as a human being, is his own. They may be those whose suffering is his own. His identification with, admiration for, and loyalty to these set up a state of conflict within him. His integrity as a human being demands the sacrifice of everything to the struggle put up on the side of free men. His integrity as a writer goes the moment he begins to write what he ought to write.

This is—whether all admit it or not—and will continue to be a particular problem for Black writers in South Africa. For them, it extends even to an orthodoxy of vocabulary: the jargon of struggle, derived internationally, is right and adequate for the public platform, the newsletter, the statement from the dock; it is not adequate, it is not deep enough, wide enough, flexible enough, cutting enough, fresh enough for the vocabulary of the poet, the short story writer or the novelist.

Neither is it, as the claim will be made, 'a language of the people' in a situation where certainly it is very important that imaginative writing must not reach the elite only. The jargon of struggle lacks both the inventive pragmatism and the poetry of common speech—those qualities the writer faces the challenge to capture and explore imaginatively, expressing as they do the soul and identity of a people as no thousandth-hand 'noble evocation' of clichés ever could.

The Black writer needs his freedom to assert that the idiom of Chatsworth, Dimbaza, Soweto is no less a vehicle for the expression of pride, self-respect, suffering, anger—or anything else in the spectrum of thought and emotion—than the language of Watts or Harlem.

The fact is, even on the side of the angels, a writer has to reserve the right to tell the truth as he sees it, in his own words, without being accused of letting the side down. For as Philip Toynbee has written, 'the writer's gift to the reader is not social zest or moral improvement or love of country, but an enlargement of the reader's apprehension'.

This is the writer's unique contribution to social change. He needs to be left alone, by brothers as well as enemies, to make this gift. And he must make it even against his own inclination.

I need hardly add this does not mean he retreats to an ivory tower. The gift cannot be made from any such place. The other day, Jean-Paul Sartre gave the following definition of the writer's responsibility to his society as an intellectual, after himself having occupied such a position in France for the best part of seventy years: 'He is someone who is faithful to a political and social body but never stops contesting it. Of course, a contradiction may arise between his fidelity and his *contestation*, but that's the fruitful contradiction. If there's fidelity with *contestation*, that's no good: one is no longer a free man.'

When a writer claims these kinds of freedom for himself, he begins to understand the real magnitude of his struggle. It is not a new problem and of all the writers who have had to face it, I don't think anyone has seen it more clearly or dealt with it with such uncompromising honesty as the great nineteenth-century Russian, Ivan Turgenev. Turgenev had an immense reputation as a progressive writer. He was closely connected with the progressive movement in Tsarist Russia and particularly with its more revolutionary wing headed by the critic Belinsky and afterwards by the poet Nekrasov. With his sketches and stories, people said that Turgenev was continuing the work Gogol had begun of awakening the conscience of the educated classes in Russia to the evils of a political regime based on serfdom.

But his friends, admirers and fellow progressives stopped short, in their understanding of his genius, of the very thing that made him one—his scrupulous reserve of the writer's freedom to reproduce truth and the reality of life, even if this truth does not coincide with his own sympathies.

When his greatest novel, *Fathers and Sons*, was published in 1862, he was attacked not only by the Right for pandering to the revolutionary nihilists, but far more bitterly by the Left, the younger generation themselves, of whom his chief character in the novel, Bazarov, was both prototype and apotheosis. The radicals and liberals, among whom Turgenev himself belonged, lambasted him as a traitor because Bazarov was presented with all the faults and contradictions that Turgenev saw in his own type, in himself, so to speak, and whom he created as he did because—in his own words—'in the given case, life happened to be like that'.

The attacks were renewed after the publication of another novel, *Smoke*, and Turgenev decided to write a series of autobiographical reminiscences which would allow him to reply to his critics by explaining his views on the art of writing, the place of the writer in society, and what the writer's attitude to the controversial problems of his day should be. The result was a series of unpretentious essays that make up a remarkable testament to a writer's creed. Dealing particularly with Bazarov and *Fathers and Sons*, he writes of his critics:

> Generally speaking they have not got quite the right idea of what is taking place in the mind of a writer or what exactly his joys and sorrows, his aims, successes and failures are. They do not, for instance, even suspect the pleasure which Gogol mentions and which consists of castigating oneself and one's faults in the imaginary characters one depicts; they are quite sure that all a writer does is to 'develop his ideas' . . . Let me illustrate my meaning by a small example. I am an inveterate and incorrigible Westerner. I have never concealed it and I am not concealing it now. And yet in spite of that it has given me great pleasure to show up in the person of Panshin [a character in *A House of Gentlefolk*] all the common and vulgar sides of the Westerners: I made the Slavophil Lavretsky 'crush him utterly'. Why did I do it, I who consider the Slavophil doctrine false and futile? Because, in the given case, *life*, according to my ideas, *happened to be like that*, and what I wanted above all was to be sincere and truthful.

And in another essay, Turgenev sums up: 'The life that surrounds him [the writer] provides him with the content of his works; he is its *concentrated reflection*; but he is as incapable of writing a panegyric as a lampoon . . . When all is said and done—that is beneath him. Only those who can do no better submit to a given theme or carry out a programme.'

A Writer's Freedom

These conditions about which I have been talking are the special, though common ones of writers beleaguered in the time of the bomb and the colour-bar, as they were in the time of the jackboot and rubber truncheon, and, no doubt, back through the ages whose shameful symbols keep tally of oppression in the skeleton cupboard of our civilizations.

Other conditions, more transient, less violent, affect the freedom of a writer's mind.

What about literary fashion, for example? What about the cycle of the innovator, the imitators, the debasers, and then the bringing forth of an innovator again? A writer must not be made too conscious of literary fashion, any more than he must allow himself to be inhibited by the mandarins, if he is to get on with work that is his own. I say 'made conscious' because literary fashion is a part of his working conditions; he can make the choice of rejecting it, but he cannot choose whether it is urged upon him or not by publishers and readers, who do not let him forget he has to eat.

That rare marvel, an innovator, should be received with shock and excitement. And his impact may set off people in new directions of their own. But the next innovator rarely, I would almost say never, comes from his imitators, those who create a fashion in his image. Not all worthwhile writing is an innovation, but I believe it always comes from an individual vision, privately pursued. The pursuit may stem from a tradition, but a tradition implies a choice of influence, whereas a fashion makes the influence of the moment the only one for all who are contemporary to it.

A writer needs all these kinds of freedom, built on the basic one of freedom from censorship. He does not ask for shelter from living, but for exposure to it without possibility of evasion. He is fiercely engaged with life on his own terms, and ought to be left to it, if anything is to come of the struggle. Any government, any society—any vision of a future society—that has respect for its writers must set them as free as possible to write in their own various ways, in their own choices of form and language, and according to their own discovery of truth.

Again, Turgenev expresses this best: 'Without freedom in the widest sense of the word—in relation to oneself . . . indeed, to one's people and one's history, a true artist is unthinkable; without that air, it is impossible to breathe.'

And I add my last word: In that air alone, commitment and creative freedom become one.

For a Cent
DON MATTERA

Don Mattera spent nine years of his life as a 'banned person' in South Africa; the banning order was unexpectedly lifted in 1982. A journalist on the Johannesburg Star *and a poet, he had thus been unable to get any of his work published in South Africa, but gained much encouragement from the publication of his poems and an excerpt from his autobiography in* Index on Censorship.

For a Cent

Each morning
        corner of Pritchard and Joubert
        leaning on a dusty crutch
        near a pavement dust-bin
        an old man begs
        not expecting much.

His spectacles are cracked and dirty
and does not see my black hand
drop a cent into his scurvy palm
but instinctively he mutters:
    Thank you my Baas!
Strange, that for a cent
a man can call his brother, Baas.

The Failure of Censorship
ANDRÉ BRINK

André Brink's book Kennis van die Aand *was banned in 1974 and was the first Afrikaans novel to meet this fate. Its English translation,* Looking on Darkness, *was also banned. This article was written for* Index on Censorship *in 1980.*

It is a cliché, but one which cannot be repeated too often, that censorship is not primarily a literary, or even a moral institution but part of the apparatus of political power: more specifically, of political power veering towards the totalitarian, and finding itself threatened from within. It is in itself an admission of fear of the written/spoken/performed *word*, which naturally lends the weight of an action to the word uttered in a closed society.

This was what the young Afrikaans writers known as the *Sestigers* ('Sixties') experienced from the moment they erupted on the scene. Even though, initially at least, our work was, in every sense of the word, 'literary', the fact that we dared to question traditional religious, moral and aesthetic values of Afrikanerdom implied the rejection of accepted authority, and it was no coincidence that censorship of a comprehensive and codified nature was first introduced in South Africa at exactly the moment the first controversial works of the *Sestigers* were published. Very soon an essentially cultural movement acquired political dimensions. The writers involved—Jan Rabie, Etienne Leroux, Breyten Breytenbach, myself and others—were branded by the establishment as 'traitors of the people'. However, their efforts to discredit us in the eyes of potential readers backfired because of the surge of enthusiasm with which especially the younger generation accepted these

The Failure of Censorship

works (even if, in the party-political field, many of these readers still supported the government). This led to an increasing wave of intimidation and eventually repression (hitherto directed mainly against English-speaking writers and, most especially, against Blacks)—a phenomenon that coincided, from the end of the 1960s, with a more overtly 'committed' form of writing in the work of a handful of Afrikaans writers. For a while it seemed as if the government—with all the 'battalions of lies' and 'organizations of fear' on their side—were heading for total victory. After the banning of my *Kennis van die Aand* (subsequently published in English as *Looking on Darkness*) in January 1974 an awesome series of bans on Afrikaans works followed, accompanied by an ever-intensifying process of harassment of Afrikaans authors (a process only too familiar to our Black colleagues and some English-speaking writers). A special section of Security Police operations was directed towards the surveillance and intimidation of writers (always bearing in mind that our lives were still easy compared to those of Black writers who could, and still can, be openly persecuted with the crudest and most brutal of means—insult, assault, detention, 'banishment', deprival of income, of social contact, or of the means to publish . . .). It begins, for the dissident writer, with the discovery that, simply *because* he is a writer, all his mail is opened and his phone tapped. And if it is relatively easy to adjust to it—and even to find in it a challenge to continue (since at the very least it suggests that one is taken seriously!)—it can become agonizing if the pressure extends to others. When a schoolteacher who innocently writes to me as a 'fan' suddenly finds herself confronted by the Security Police and threatened with the loss of her job *simply because she has written to me*, it places a terrible burden not only on her conscience but on mine as well.

There is the strain of constant surveillance (even when one goes on an ordinary family outing); it is an eye-opening experience to return from a journey abroad and to be confronted, on the plane, by an individual who blandly gives one a catalogue of all the details of the trip and all the people one has met; and who concludes his chat with the wry announcement: 'Welcome back to South Africa.'

But of course one learns to live with that, as one learns to cope with the anonymous threats, by letter or telephone, against the members of one's family. If one is not prepared to live with it, one should either heed the censor or not write at all. There are other methods too, all of them extensions of censorship: an 'invitation' to visit the Special Branch and 'discuss things'; and next time *they* are the visitors, arriving unannounced and with a great show of strength, to search one's house and confiscate notes and correspondence and even one's typewriters. (And six months later Steve Biko dies and one recognizes among the names of his interrogators some of those who 'visited' one's own home.)

And all the time, obviously, censorship proper runs its course: books are either banned or placed under a 'temporary' embargo (up to six months—in the hope, presumably, that public interest will die down). And surrounding the workings of 'official' censorship there is the climate of fear and uncertainty surrounding it: one's regular publisher turns down a book for fear of a *possible* ban; a printer refuses to print a novel for fear of being implicated *in case* it is banned; booksellers decline to buy stocks of 'dubious' titles. (And in the long run, the censor hopes, the writer himself, especially if he is young and vulnerable and eager to see himself in print, may start doing the censor's dirty work for him.)

And yet I believe that censorship in South Africa has failed, and quite spectacularly so, as should be clear from a brief look at some of the aspects involved:

1. Censorship tries to inhibit written opposition to the system. In South Africa this has, admittedly, succeeded up to a point. After the explosion of new talent in fiction in the

1960s the ensuing decade brought only one truly important new name in Afrikaans (John Miles); and one in English (J. M. Coetzee); and state-subsidized theatre, in spite of splendiferous new buildings and amenities, is almost moribund. But this is not the total picture. In Black writing the past decade has seen an eruption of talent and vitality unrivalled in South African literary history. Much of it is banned—but most of it gets distributed in a wide variety of ways before a ban is imposed; and poetry readings and fly-by-night performances of plays reach an increasing audience. In fact, Black writing has become one of the most important factors pushing for change (and *directing* that change) in South Africa.

Also, to compensate for the paucity of new voices among White writers, existing ones have acquired an increasing audience both in South Africa and abroad. My own experience may point to a larger trend: not only do my books sell more copies in South Africa than before they were hit by the censors (and banned books, too, continue to circulate at a dizzy pace), but the threat of being censored in Afrikaans, which would effectively deprive me of my habitual readers, prompted me, as a measure of literary survival, to start writing in English as well. The result is that books previously available only in Afrikaans are now published in some twenty different countries. (And because they are in English they are now, for the first time, being read by Black readers in South Africa too, as well as being translated into indigenous languages.) In several countries a new awareness of South African writing has grown precisely because of the publicity given to the workings of censorship.

2. Censorship is aimed at isolating writers from one another through fear and intimidation. In South Africa the opposite has happened. For a very long time three different streams of literature ran their separate courses: Black, Afrikaans and English. But during the last few years a new awareness of a

common identity as writers has arisen, creating a new sense of solidarity in a body of informed and articulate resistance to oppression. The establishment of a Soweto-based PEN Centre was a culminating point in this development. It is true that the Centre was recently closed down—in itself an ominous and depressing symptom of the deteriorating situation in the country—but one should not misjudge the event. Black writers turned away from PEN because of pressure from their society and their commitment to that society, *not* because as writers they themselves rejected co-operation with Whites. In fact, in many ways and on many levels the association of writers of different races and cultures continues, and it is intensified by the awareness of a common enemy.

It would be naïve to ascribe increased opposition to apartheid to censorship only but in a complex situation censorship has become a significant catalyst in creating solidarity and in deepening awareness.

3. Censorship wants to alienate reader and writer from each other. Far from achieving this, censorship in South Africa has created for the reader a new sense of adventure in literature, a new sense of being 'in touch'. This is illustrated by the increased demand for banned books among White readers and in the way in which new publications by Blacks are sold on the streets of Soweto. When *Kennis van die Aand* was banned the public rallied by collecting thousands of pounds (most of it contributed in sums of two or three pounds by anonymous donors, 'ordinary readers') in order to fight the ban in the courts.

4. Censorship tries to reduce the writer to a state of impotence. But the establishment of a variety of writers' organizations (with the Afrikaans Writers Guild, open to all languages and races, the most influential among them) testifies to the frustration of this aim. Writers have acquired

a larger and more effective public forum since the introduction of censorship than ever before.

There is another telling example of the failure of censorship on this point: the fund referred to above, established to fight the ban on *Kennis van die Aand*, was in fact used to launch the small private publishing enterprise *Taurus* which publishes any manuscript that runs the risk of being banned. A list of subscribers was even established and when, in 1979, it became obvious that my novel *A Dry White Season* was in danger of being banned (in its Afrikaans version), two thousand copies were quietly printed and despatched to *Taurus* subscribers, followed by another edition within a week. By the time the censors pounced there were enough copies in circulation to ensure a long clandestine existence; at the same time writers declared themselves prepared to take the plunge into full samizdat unless the government changed its censorship policies — not only towards the books of a few token authors but towards South African publications in general. This may or may not have contributed to the fact that Nadine Gordimer's *Burger's Daughter* was 'unbanned' a few months later, followed by my *Dry White Season* and Etienne Leroux's *Magersfontein*—and, most significantly, by Mothobi Mutloatse's *Forced Landing* soon after.

The important thing was that a psychological victory had been gained and that, from now on, even young writers knew that their work could be published, whether 'bannable' or not.

It is obvious that, with the formidable apparatus at its disposal, the government may close up existing loopholes in due course. But the writers now have the advantage of a head start and of having seen the power of the written word in action. At the same time censorship has failed to neutralize the writers, as a result of increasing international recognition of the work of some authors: which may not provide total 'protection', should the government really decide to clamp down, but which certainly undermines both the efficacy of censorship and the credibility of the government behind it.

5. Censorship is based on the concern to impose an ideology at the expense of the free circulation of ideas. And obviously South African society has been sadly impoverished through lack of open contact with the ideas of the world outside. But at the same time censorship stimulates interest in what is banned. And the enthusiastic reception of work by dissident writers by the younger generation of readers (of all races) counters much of the ravages of censorship. If a young Afrikaner writes to me that 'after reading your book I realize for the first time that Blacks are human beings just like us', it is more than a shattering admission of what apartheid does to people; it also announces the stirring of that individual questioning and revolt where all social revolutions begin.

The writer does not primarily direct himself at 'changing the system' but at awakening the individual consciousness in such a way that eventually a change in the 'system' becomes not only possible but inevitable. And the existence of censorship is aiding the process by lending greater resonance to the words of writers.

6. Censorship aims at maintaining the unity of the 'system'. In South Africa the banning of certain works (notably Leroux's *Magersfontein*) has already placed some fervent disciples of the government in an unbearable situation — loyal to the politics of the government they yet find themselves constrained to defend both the aesthetics and the morality of a banned work. If one government body bans a book and another awards it a prestigious literary prize, schizophrenia sets in and another crack appears on the granite face of the 'system'.

7. Censorship is humourless. It cannot be otherwise. Yet few institutions in recent South African history have been so devastatingly ridiculed—not only by opponents but from within the laager itself—as censorship. The system has not been helped, either, by some of the personalities administering it or by some of the farcical contradictions in their decisions.

One should not rejoice too soon. Much harm can still be done. Censorship has demonstrated its own failure but it is not yet dead. And a hardening of political attitudes may well result in a new and even more draconian application of its apparatus. Still, its failure is already an historical fact—provided writers continue to expose it for what it is and to fight it every inch of the way: with courage, with perseverance, and not without a healthy sense of humour.

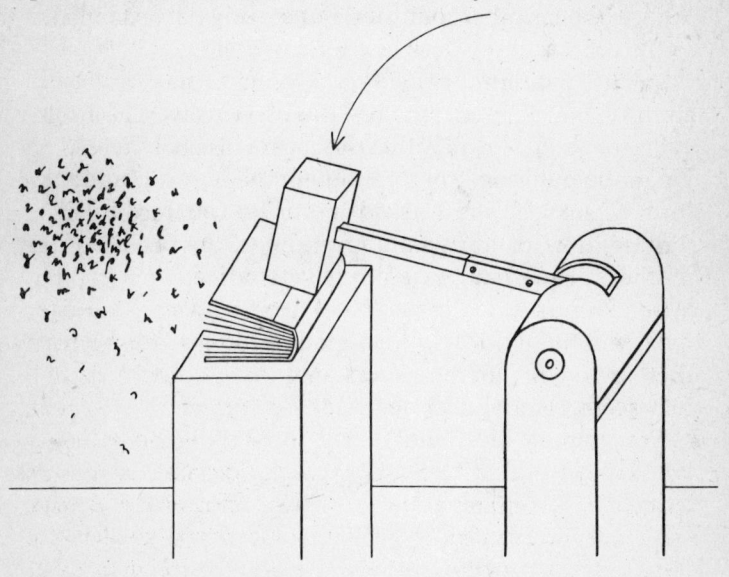

Comedy is Everywhere
MILAN KUNDERA

Milan Kundera left Czechoslovakia in 1975 and lived for a time in Rennes before settling in Paris. His novel, The Book of Laughter and Forgetting, *established his reputation as a foremost European writer. The following is the text of an interview he gave to George Theiner for* Index on Censorship *in Rennes in 1977.*

I am certainly in a rather odd situation. I write my novels in Czech. But since 1970 I have not been allowed to publish in my own country, and so no one reads me in that language. My books are first translated into French and published in France, then in other countries, but the original text remains in the drawer of my desk as a kind of matrix.

In the autumn of 1968 in Vienna I met a fellow-countryman, a writer, who had decided to leave Czechoslovakia for good. He knew that this meant his books would no longer be published there. I thought he was committing a form of suicide, and I asked him if he was reconciled to writing only for translators in future, if the beauty of his mother tongue had ceased to have any meaning for him. When I returned to Prague, I had two surprises in store for me: even though I didn't emigrate, I too was forced from then on to write for translators only. And, paradoxical as it may seem, I feel it has done my mother tongue a lot of good.

Conciseness and clarity are, for me, what makes a language beautiful. Czech is a vivid, suggestive, sensuous language, sometimes at the expense of a firm order, logical sequence and exactitude. It contains a strong poetic element, but it is difficult to convey all its meanings to a foreign reader. I am very concerned that I should be translated faithfully. Writing my last two novels, I particularly had my French translator in mind. I made myself—at first unknowingly—write sentences that were more sober, more comprehensible. A cleansing of the language. I have a great affection for the eighteenth century. So much the better then if my Czech sentences have to peer carefully into the clear mirror of Diderot's tongue.

Goethe once said to Eckermann that they were witnessing the end of national literature and the birth of a world literature. I am convinced that a literature aimed solely at a national readership has, since Goethe's time, been an anachronism and fails to fulfil its basic function. To depict human situations in a way which makes it impossible for them to be understood beyond the frontiers of any single country is a disservice to the readers of that country too. By so doing we prevent them from looking further than their own backyard, we force them into a straitjacket of parochialism. Not to have one's work published in one's own country is a cruel lesson, but I think a useful one. In our times we must consider a book that is unable to become part of the world's literature to be non-existent.

As a Czech writer I don't like being pigeon-holed in the literature of Eastern Europe. Eastern Europe is a purely political term barely thirty years old. As far as cultural tradition is concerned, Eastern Europe is Russia, whereas Prague belongs to Central Europe. Unfortunately, West Europeans don't know their geography. This ignorance could be fatal, as indeed it has proved to be in the past. Remember Chamberlain in 1938 and his words about 'a small country we know little about'.

The nations of Central Europe are small and far too well concealed behind a barrier of languages which no one knows and few study. And yet it is this very part of Europe which, over the past fifty years, has become a kind of crucible in which history has carried out incredible experiments, both with individuals and with nations. And the fact that those living in Western Europe have only very simplified notions, have never taken the trouble properly to study what is going on a few hundred kilometres from their own tranquil homes can, I repeat, be fatal to them.

From this Central Europe have come several major cultural impulses, without which our century would be unthinkable: Freud's psychoanalysis; Schönberg's dodecaphony; the novels of Kafka and Hašek, which have discovered a grotesque new literary world and the new poetry of the non-psychological novel; and finally structuralism, born and developed in Prague in the twenties, to become a fashion in West Europe thirty years later. I grew up with these traditions and have little in common with Eastern Europe. Forgive me if I seem to dwell on these ridiculous geographical details.

Large nations are obsessed with the idea of unification. They see progress in unity. Even President Carter's message to the inhabitants of outer space contains a passage expressing regret that the world is as yet divided into nations and the hope that it will soon come together in a single civilization. As if unity were a cure for all ills. A small nation, in its efforts to maintain its very existence, fights for its right to be different. If unification is progress, then small nations are anti-progressive to the core, in the finest sense of the word.

Big nations make history, small ones receive its blessings. Big nations consider themselves the masters of history and thus cannot but take history, and themselves, seriously. A small nation does not see history as its property and has a right not to take it seriously.

Franz Kafka was a Jew, Jaroslav Hašek a Czech—both members of a minority. When the First World War broke out, Europe was seized by a paroxysm of warlike nationalism, which did not spare even Thomas Mann or Apollinaire. In Franz Kafka's diary we can read: 'Germany has declared war on Russia. Went swimming in the afternoon.'

And when, in 1914, Hašek's Schweik learns that Ferdinand has been killed, he asks which one—the barber's apprentice who once drank some hair oil, or was it the Ferdinand who collects dogshit on the pavement?

They say the greatness of life is to be found only where life transcends itself. But what if all transcendent life is history —which does not belong to us anyway? Is there only Kafka's absurd office? Only the daftness of Hašek's army? Where then is the greatness, the gravity, the meaning of it all? The genius of the minorities has discovered its *grotesqueness*. Hegel's concept of history — wise and ascending, like assiduous schoolgirls, ever higher on the staircase of progress—has been inconspicuously buried by Hašek and Kafka. In this sense we are their heirs.

Our Prague humour is often difficult to understand. The critics took Miloš Forman to task because in one of his films he made the audience laugh where they shouldn't. Where it was out of place. But isn't that just what it is all about? Comedy isn't here simply to stay docilely in the drawer allotted to comedies, farces and entertainments, where 'serious spirits' would confine it. Comedy is everywhere, in each one of us, it goes with us like our shadow, it is even in our misfortune, lying in wait for us like a precipice. Joseph K. is comic because of his disciplined obedience, and his story is all the more tragic for it. Hašek laughs in the midst of terrible massacres, and these become all the more unbearable as a result. You see, there is consolation in tragedy. Tragedy gives us an illusion of greatness and meaning. People who have led tragic lives can speak of this with pride. Those who lack the tragic dimension, who have known only the comedies of life, can have no illusions about themselves.

When I came to France, the thing that astonished me most was the difference in national humour. The French are immensely humorous, witty, gay. But they take themselves and the world seriously. We are far more sad, but we take nothing seriously.

All my life in Czechoslovakia I fought against literature being reduced to a mere instrument of propaganda. Then I found myself in the West only to discover that here people write about the literature of the so-called East European countries as if it were indeed nothing more than a propaganda instrument, be it pro- or anti-communist. I must confess I don't like the word 'dissident', particularly when applied to art. It is part and parcel of that same politicizing, ideological distortion which cripples a work of art. The novels of Tibor Déry, Miloš Forman's films—are they dissident or aren't they? They cannot be fitted into such a category. If you cannot view the art that comes to you from Prague or Budapest in any other way than by means of this idiotic political code, you murder it no less brutally than the worst of the Stalinist dogmatists. And you are quite unable to hear its true voice. The importance of this art does not lie in the fact that it accuses this or that political regime, but in the fact that, on the strength of social and human experience of a kind people over here cannot even imagine, it offers new testimony about the human condition.

If by 'committed' you mean literature in the service of a certain political creed, then let me tell you straight that such a literature is mere conformity of the worst kind.

A writer always envies a boxer or a revolutionary. He longs for action and, wishing to take a direct part in 'real' life, makes his work serve immediate political aims. The nonconformity of the novel, however, does not lie in its identification with a radical, opposition political line, but in presenting a different, independent, unique view of the world. Thus, and only thus, can the novel attack conventional opinions and attitudes.

There are commentators who are obsessed with the demon of simplification. They murder books by reducing them to a mere political interpretation. Such people are only interested in so-called 'Eastern' writers as long as their books are banned. As far as they're concerned, there are official writers and opposition writers—and that is all. They forget that any genuine literature eludes this sort of evaluation, that it eludes the Manichaeism of propaganda.

We have got into the habit of putting the blame for everything on 'regimes'. This enables us not to see that a regime only sets in motion mechanisms which already exist in ourselves. . . . A novel's mission is not to pillory evident political realities but to expose anthropological scandals.

To speak of the end of the novel is a local preoccupation of West European writers, notably the French. It's absurd to talk about it to a writer from my part of Europe, or from Latin America. How can one possibly mumble something about the death of the novel and have on one's bookshelf *One Hundred Years of Solitude* by Gabriel García Márquez? As long as there is human experience which cannot be depicted except in a novel, all conjectures about its having expired are mere expressions of snobbery. It is, of course, possibly true to say that the novel in Western Europe no longer provides many new insights and that for those we have to look to the other part of Europe and to Latin America.

The novel is a game with invented characters. You see the world through their eyes, and thus you see it from various angles. The more differentiated the characters, the more the author and the reader have to step outside themselves and try to understand. Ideology wants to convince you that its truth is absolute. A novel shows you that everything is relative. Ideology is a school of intolerance. A novel teaches you tolerance and understanding. The more ideological our century becomes, the more anachronistic is the novel. But the more anachronistic it gets, the more we need it. Today, when politics have become a religion, I see the novel as one of the last forms of atheism.

A true novel always stands beyond hope and despair. Hope is not a value, merely an unproven supposition that things will get better. A novel gives you something far better than hope. A novel gives you joy. The joy of imagination, of narration, the joy provided by a game. That is how I see a novel—as a game.

Of course, if the game is to be worthwhile, it must be played and must be about something serious. It must be a game with fire and demons. The game of the novel combines the lightest and the hardest, the most serious with the most lighthearted.

You Have Insulted Me: a Letter
KURT VONNEGUT

As recently as 1973 Kurt Vonnegut's novel Slaughterhouse Five *was consigned to the flames in a school furnace in North Dakota. Books written by Vonnegut and other leading American authors such as Bernard Malamud, James Dickey and Joseph Heller are 'regularly thrown out of school libraries'. Vonnegut's letter to the chairman of the school board in Drake, North Dakota, comes from his book,* Palm Sunday *(Delacorte Press/Seymour Lawrence, 1981; Jonathan Cape, 1981).*

My novel *Slaughterhouse Five* was actually burned in a furnace by a school janitor in Drake, North Dakota, on instructions from the school committee there, and the school board made public statements about the unwholesomeness of the book. Even by the standards of Queen Victoria, the only offensive line in the entire novel is this: 'Get out of the road, you dumb motherfucker.' This is spoken by an American antitank gunner to an unarmed American chaplain's assistant during the Battle of the Bulge in Europe in December 1944, the largest single defeat of American arms (the Confederacy excluded) in history. The chaplain's assistant had attracted enemy fire.

So on 16 November 1973 I wrote as follows to Charles McCarthy of Drake, North Dakota:

Dear Mr McCarthy:
I am writing to you in your capacity as chairman of the Drake School Board. I am among those American writers whose books have been destroyed in the now famous furnace of your school.

Certain members of your community have suggested that

my work is evil. This is extraordinarily insulting to me. The news from Drake indicates to me that books and writers are very unreal to you people. I am writing this letter to let you know how real I am.

I want you to know, too, that my publisher and I have done absolutely nothing to exploit the disgusting news from Drake. We are not clapping each other on the back, crowing about all the books we will sell because of the news. We have declined to go on television, have written no fiery letters to editorial pages, have granted no lengthy interviews. We are angered and sickened and saddened. And no copies of this letter have been sent to anybody else. You now hold the only copy in your hands. It is a strictly private letter from me to the people of Drake, who have done so much to damage my reputation in the eyes of their children and then in the eyes of the world. Do you have the courage and ordinary decency to show this letter to the people, or will it, too, be consigned to the fires of your furnace?

I gather from what I read in the papers and hear on television that you imagine me, and some other writers, too, as being sort of ratlike people who enjoy making money from poisoning the minds of young people. I am in fact a large, strong person, fifty-one years old, who did a lot of farm work as a boy, who is good with tools. I have raised six children, three my own and three adopted. They have all turned out well. Two of them are farmers. I am a combat infantry veteran from World War II and hold a Purple Heart. I have earned whatever I own by hard work. I have never been arrested or sued for anything. I am so much trusted with young people and by young people that I have served on the faculties of the University of Iowa, Harvard, and the City College of New York. Every year I receive at least a dozen invitations to be commencement speaker at colleges and high schools. My books are probably more widely used in schools than those of any other living American fiction writer.

You Have Insulted Me: a Letter

If you were to bother to read my books, to behave as educated persons would, you would learn that they are not sexy, and do not argue in favour of wildness of any kind. They beg that people be kinder and more responsible than they often are. It is true that some of the characters speak coarsely. That is because people speak coarsely in real life. Especially soldiers and hard working men speak coarsely, and even our most sheltered children know that. And we all know, too, that those words really don't damage children much. They didn't damage us when we were young. It was evil deeds and lying that hurt us.

After I have said all this, I am sure you are still ready to respond, in effect, 'Yes, yes—but it still remains our right and our responsibility to decide what books our children are going to be made to read in our community.' This is surely so. But it is also true that if you exercise that right and fulfil that responsibility in an ignorant, harsh, un-American manner, then people are entitled to call you bad citizens and fools. Even your own children are entitled to call you that.

I read in the newspaper that your community is mystified by the outcry from all over the country about what you have done. Well, you have discovered that Drake is a part of American civilization, and your fellow Americans can't stand it that you have behaved in such an uncivilized way. Perhaps you will learn from that that books are sacred to free men for very good reasons, and that wars have been fought against nations which hate books and burn them. If you are an American, you must allow all ideas to circulate freely in your community, not merely your own.

If you and your board are now determined to show that you in fact have wisdom and maturity when you exercise your powers over the education of your young, then you should acknowledge that it was a rotten lesson you taught young people in a free society when you denounced and then burned books—books you hadn't even read. You should also resolve to expose your children to all sorts of opinions and information, in order that they will be better equipped to make decisions and to survive.

Again: you have insulted me, and I am a good citizen, and I am very real.

That was seven years ago. There has so far been no reply. At this very moment, as I write in New York City, *Slaughterhouse Five* has been banned from school libraries not fifty miles from here. A legal battle begun several years ago rages on. The school board in question has found lawyers eager to attack the First Amendment tooth and nail. There is never a shortage anywhere of lawyers eager to attack the First Amendment, as though it were nothing more than a clause in a lease from a crooked slumlord.

The Writer in Latin America
MARIO VARGAS LLOSA

Mario Vargas Llosa, the Peruvian novelist and former President of International PEN, gave this paper at the University of Oklahoma in 1977. It appeared in Index on Censorship *in 1978.*

The Peruvian novelist José María Arguedas killed himself on the second day of December 1969 in a classroom of La Molina Agricultural University in Lima. He was a very discreet man, and so as not to disturb his colleagues and the students with his suicide, he waited until everybody had left the place. Near his body was found a letter with very detailed instructions about his burial.

But some days later other letters written by him appeared, little by little. They too were different aspects of his last will, and they were addressed to very different people; his publisher, friends, journalists, academics, politicians. The main subject of these letters was his death, of course, or better, the reasons for which he decided to kill himself. These reasons changed from letter to letter. In one of them he said that he had decided to commit suicide because he felt that he was finished as a writer, that he no longer had the impulse and the will to create. In another he gave moral, social and political reasons: he could no longer stand the misery and neglect of the Peruvian peasants, those people of the Indian communities among whom he had been raised; he lived oppressed and anguished by the crises of the cultural and educational life in the country; the low level and abject nature of the press and the caricature of liberty in Peru were too much for him, et cetera.

In these dramatic letters we follow, naturally, the personal crises that Arguedas had been going through, and they are the desperate call of a suffering man who, at the edge of the abyss, asks mankind for help and compassion. But they are not only that: a clinical testimony. At the same time, they are graphic evidence of the situation of the writer in Latin America, of the difficulties and pressures of all sorts that have surrounded and disoriented and many times destroyed the literary vocation in our countries.

In the USA, in Western Europe, to be a writer means, generally, first (and usually only) to assume a personal responsibility. That is, the responsibility to achieve in the most rigorous and authentic way a work which, for its artistic values and originality, enriches the language and culture of one's country. In Peru, in Bolivia, in Nicaragua et cetera, on the contrary, to be a writer means, at the same time, to assume a social responsibility: at the same time that you develop a personal literary work, you should serve, through your writing but also through your actions, as an active participant in the solution of the economic, political and cultural problems of your society. There is no way to escape this obligation. If you tried to do so, if you were to isolate yourself and concentrate exclusively on your own work, you would be severely censured and considered, in the best of cases, irresponsible and selfish, or at worst, even by omission, an accomplice to all the evils—illiteracy, misery, exploitation, injustice, prejudice—of your country and against which you have refused to fight. In the letters which he wrote once he had prepared the gun with which he was to kill himself, Arguedas was trying, in the last moments of his life, to fulfil this moral imposition that impels all Latin American writers to social and political commitment.

Why is it like this? The answer lies in the social condition of Latin America, the problems which face our countries. All countries have problems, of course, but in many parts of Latin America, both in the past and in the present, the problems which constitute the closest daily reality for people are not freely discussed and analysed in public, but are usually denied and silenced. There are no means through which those problems can be presented and denounced, because the social and political establishment exercises a strict censorship of the media and over all the communications systems. For example, if today you hear Chilean broadcasts or see Argentine television, you won't hear a word about the political prisoners, about the exiles, about the torture, about the violations of human rights in those two countries that have outraged the conscience of the world. You will, however, be carefully informed, of course, about the iniquities of the communist countries. If you read the daily newspapers of my country, for instance —which have been confiscated by the government, which now controls them—you will not find a word about the arrests of labour leaders or about the murderous inflation that affects everyone. You will read only about what a happy and prosperous country Peru is and how much we Peruvians love our military rulers.

What happens with the press, TV and radio happens too, most of the time, with the universities. The government persistently interferes with them; teachers and students considered subversive or hostile to the official system are expelled and the whole curriculum reorganized according to political considerations. As an indication of what extremes of absurdity this 'cultural policy' can reach, you must remember, for instance, that in Argentina, in Chile and in Uruguay the Departments of Sociology have been closed indefinitely, because the social sciences are considered subversive. Academic knowledge in many Latin American countries is, like the press and the media, a victim of the deliberate turning away from what is actually happening in society. This vacuum has been filled by literature.

So, something curious and paradoxical occurred. The realm of imagination became in Latin America the kingdom of objective reality; fiction became a substitute for social science; our best teachers about reality were the dreamers, the literary artists.

The participation of the Latin American writer in the social and political evaluation of reality has been decisive. Frequently, and often very effectively, he has taken the place of the scientist, the journalist and the social agitator in carrying out this mission. He has thus helped to establish a conception of literature which has penetrated all sectors. Literature, according to this view, appears as a meaningful and positive activity, which depicts the scars of reality and prescribes remedies, frustrating official lies so that the truth shines through. It is also directed towards the future: it demands and predicts social change (revolution), that new society, freed from the evil spirits which literature denounces and exorcizes with words. According to this conception, imagination and language are entirely at the service of the civic ideal, and literature is as subordinate to objective reality as history books (or even more so, for the reasons already discussed). This vision of literature as a mimetic enterprise, morally uplifting, historically fruitful, sociologically exact, politically revolutionary, has become so widespread in our countries that it partly explains the irrational behaviour of many of the dictatorships of the continent. Hardly installed in power, they persecute, imprison, torture and even kill writers who often have had no political involvement, as was the case in Uruguay, Chile and Argentina not long ago.* The mere fact of being a writer makes them suspicious, a threat in the short or long term to

---

*The fact that this persecution is carried out against the person of the writer, not against his books, is symptomatic of what I am saying. During the dictatorship of Odria in Peru (1948–56) the leaders of APRA (Popular Alliance for the American Revolution) and communist leaders were severely repressed, but you could buy the essays of Haya de la Torre (leader of APRA) and Jose Carlos Mariategui (founder of the Peruvian Communist Party). Today in Argentina, the books of Haroldo Conti and Rodolfo Walsh are still in circulation, while the authors themselves have disappeared and may be dead.

the status quo. All this adds considerably to the complexity of something which in itself is difficult to explain, the misunderstanding at the back of all this.

The 'commitment' of a writer, understood as the obligation to take account of the injustices in his world and to think in terms of solutions, is no guarantee that his work has artistic value. The writer who aims to break the silence around social problems and to demand solutions is not necessarily original or creative. But on the other hand, once this conception of literature is established in the minds of the public, it makes it more difficult to dissociate the one from the other: literary merit and the social and political effectiveness of a text. A society convinced that literature must be useful—that it must serve the present—will find it difficult to understand or accept those works which instead of reproducing reality, seek to order it or deny it. Nevertheless, the latter constitutes true literature. For society to accept them, if it dare not reject them altogether, the critics must distort them, present them as symbols or allegories, which appear as magic, or fantasy or insanity, but also fulfil the edifying mission of denouncing evil and propagating good.

As André Gide once said, good sentiments do not usually generate good literature. Perhaps the phrase could be reworded to state that, more often, good sentiments do not produce literature, but something different: religion, ethics, politics, philosophy, history, journalism. Literature can make use of all these to achieve its ends, that's clear—it is always doing so—but, on the other hand, it can only serve them by selling its soul, becoming that which wants to serve. Because literature does not demonstrate but illuminates, ideas are less important in it than obsessions and intuitions. Its truth does not depend on its coincidence with reality, but on its ability to distinguish itself from it. It is not only indifferent to the present, but is aware of it only inasmuch as it transcends it and takes root in something more permanent. Its origins are much more in the troubled, prohibited depths of human experience than in any prophylactic social voluntarism. And the service which it really does for man, is not to contribute to the propagation of the faith and the catechism (religious or political), but precisely in undermining the very foundations on which all faith rests, and in testing (that is relativizing) all rationalist knowledge of the world. The congenital unsubmissiveness of literature is much broader than is believed by those who consider it a mere instrument for opposing governments and dominant social structures: it strikes equally at everything which stands for dogma and logical exclusivism in the interpretation of life, that is both ideological orthodoxies and heterodoxies. *In other words, it is a living, systematic, inevitable contradiction of all that exists.*

In one sense people—the real or potential readers of the writer—are accustomed to considering literature as something intimately associated with living and social problems, the activity through which all that is repressed or disfigured in society will be named, described and condemned. They expect novels, poems and plays to counterbalance the policy of disguising and deforming reality which is current in the official culture and to keep alive the hope and spirit of change and revolt among the victims of that policy. In another sense this confers on the writer, as a citizen, a kind of moral and spiritual leadership, and he must try, during his life as a writer, to act according to this image of the role he is expected to play. Of course he can reject it and refuse this task that society wants to impose on him; and declaring that he does not want to be either a politician or a moralist or a sociologist, but only an artist, he can seclude himself in his personal dreams. However, this will be considered (and in a way, it is) a political, a moral and a social choice. He will be considered by his real and potential readers as a deserter and a traitor, and his poems, novels and plays will be endangered. To be an artist, only an artist, can become in our countries, a kind of moral crime, a political sin. All our literature is marked by this fact, and if this is not taken into consideration, one cannot fully understand all the differences that exist between it and other literatures of the world.

No writer in Latin America is unaware of the pressure that is put on him, pushing him to a social commitment. Some accept this because the external impulse coincides with their innermost feelings and personal convictions. These cases are, surely, the happy ones. It is interesting to note that many Latin American men and women whose writing started out as totally uncommitted, indifferent or even hostile to social problems and politics, later—sometimes gradually, sometimes abruptly—orientated their writings in this direction. The reason for this change could be, of course, that they adopted new attitudes, acknowledging the terrible social problems of our countries, an intellectual discovery of the evils of society and the moral decision to fight them. But we cannot dismiss the possibility that in this change (conscious or unconscious) the psychological and practical trouble it means for a writer to resist the social pressure for political commitment also played a role, as did the psychological and practical advantages which led him to act and to write as society expects him to.

It is worth noting too that the political commitment of writers and literature in Latin America is a result not only of the social abuse and economic exploitation of large sectors of the population by small minorities and brutal military dictatorships. There are also cultural reasons for this commitment, exigencies that the writer himself sees grow and take root in his conscience during and because of his artistic development. To be a writer, to discover this vocation and to choose to practise it pushes one inevitably, in our countries, to discover all the handicaps and miseries of underdevelopment. Inequities, injustice, exploitation, discrimination, abuse are not only the burden of peasants, workers, employees, minorities. They are also social obstacles for the development of a cultural life. How can literature exist in a society where the rates of illiteracy reach 50 or 60 per cent of the population? How can literature exist in countries where there are no publishing houses, where there are no literary publications, where if you want to publish a book you must finance it yourself? How can a cultural and literary life develop in a society where the material conditions of life—lack of education, subsistence wages et cetera—establish a kind of cultural apartheid, that is, prevent the majority of the inhabitants from buying and reading books? And if, besides all that, the political authorities have established a rigid censorship in the press, in the media and in the universities, that is, in those places through which literature would normally find encouragement and an audience, how could the Latin American writer remain indifferent to social and political problems?

We can say that there are some positive aspects in this kind of situation for literature. Because of that commitment, literature is forced to keep in touch with living reality, with the experiences of people, and it is prevented from becoming—as unfortunately has happened in some developed societies—an esoteric and ritualistic experimentation in new forms of expression almost entirely dissociated from real experience. And because of social commitment, writers are obliged to be socially responsible for what they write and for what they do, because social pressure provides a firm barrier against the temptation of using words and imagination in order to play the game of moral irresponsibility, the game of the *enfant terrible* who (only at the level of words, of course) cheats, lies, exaggerates and proposes the worst options.

In this context, the printed word, the written word, the book, have a privileged position, deserve respect and encourage hope. They enjoy total credibility. The pressures put on the pen presuppose that it is capable of telling the truth, of accurately reproducing the real, dispelling ambiguities and that novels, poems, plays can—like bombs, earthquakes and miracles—produce instantaneous and profound social change, destroying all that is bad. This belief in the omnipotence of literature in the socio-political realm is ingenuous, but ensures it a more elevated function than that of mere entertainment, and that can be a powerful stimulus for the writer. It is a belief which rests on a real and salutary fact. In Latin America books have not been controlled, manipulated and debased by those in power as have other means of expression. In the majority of countries, literature continues to be the final bastion of freedom. That is due to the fortunate stupidity of governments, who have not considered literature harmful enough to merit censorship. But also because of the nature of literary creativity, the loneliness in which it is born, the relative ease with which it is reproduced and circulated, and the lasting impression it makes when men recognize themselves in it, amongst human creations, the one which has shown most resistance to bowing down before authority, which has best avoided its onslaughts. These days when prophets emerge in so many places to announce its death, it is consoling that literature has been and continues to be associated with these longings: that truth be spoken and injustice suppressed.

But this situation has many dangers, too. The function and the practice of literature can be entirely distorted if creative writing is seen only (or even mainly) as the materialization of social and political aims. What is to be, then, the borderline, the frontier between history, sociology and literature? Are we going to say that literature is only a degraded form (since its data are always dubious because of the place that fantasy occupies in it) of the social sciences? In fact, this is what literature becomes if its most praised value is considered to be the testimony it offers of objective reality, if it is judged principally as a true record of what happens in society.

On the other hand, this opens the door of literature to all kinds of opportunistic attitudes and intellectual blackmail. How can I condemn as an artistic failure a novel that explicitly protests against the oppressors of the masses without being considered an accomplice of the oppressor? How can I say that this poem which fulminates in assonant verses against the great corporations is a calamity without being considered an obsequious servant of imperialism? And we know how this kind of simplistic approach to literature can be utilized by dishonest intellectuals and imposed easily on uneducated audiences.

The exigency of social commitment can signify also the destruction of artistic vocations in that, because of the particular sensibility, experiences and temperament of a writer, he is unable to accomplish in his writings and actions what society expects of him. The realm of sensibility, of human experience and of imagination is wider than the realm of politics and social problems. A writer like Borges has built a great literary work of art in which this kind of problem is entirely ignored: metaphysics, philosophy, fantasy and literature are more important for him. (But he has been unable to keep himself from answering the social call for commitment, and one is tempted to see in his incredible statements on right-wing conservatism—statements that scare even the conservatives—just a strategy of political sacrilege in order not to be disturbed once and for all in his writings.) And many writers are not really prepared to deal with political and social problems. These are the unhappy cases. If they prefer their intimate call and produce uncommitted work, they will have to face all kinds of misunderstanding and rejection. Incomprehension and hostility will be their constant reward. If they submit to social pressure and try to write about social and political themes, it is quite probable that they will fail as writers, that they will frustrate themselves as artists for not having acted as their feelings prompted them to do.

I think that José María Arguedas experienced this terrible dilemma and that all his life and work bears the trace of it. He was born in the Andes, was raised among the Indian peasants (in spite of being the son of a lawyer) and, until his adolescence, was—in the language he spoke and in his vision of the world—an Indian. Later he was recaptured by his family and became a middle-class Spanish-speaking Peruvian White. He lived torn always between these two different cultures and societies. And literature meant for him, in his first short stories and novels, a melancholic escape to the days and places of his childhood, the world of the little Indian villages—San Juan de Lucanas, Puquio—or towns of the Andes such as Abancay, whose landscapes and customs he described in a tender and poetic prose. But later he felt obliged to renounce this kind of lyric image to fulfil the social responsibilities that everybody expected of him. And he wrote a very ambitious book, *Todas las sangres* (1964), in which he tried to describe the social and political problems of his country. The novel is a total failure: the vision is simplistic, a caricature. We find none of the great literary virtues that made of his previous books genuine works of art. The book is the classic failure of an artistic talent due to the self-imposition of social commitment. The other books of Arguedas oscillate between those two sides of his personality, and it is probable that all this played a part in his suicide.

When he pressed the trigger of the gun, at the University of La Molina, on the second day of December in 1969, José María Arguedas was too, in a way, showing how difficult and daring it can be to be a writer in Latin America.

Something More than Words
JULIO CORTÁZAR

Julio Cortázar, a prominent Argentinian writer living in France, was one of the speakers at a conference of International PEN in Stockholm in May 1978. The text of his speech, from which the following piece is taken, was published in Index on Censorship *in 1978. Julio Cortázar died in Paris on 12 February, 1984.*

Almost every significant message reaches the public by way of writing; discussion among us, the intellectuals, is useful and necessary, but what is really important today is the slow projection of everything into the consciousness of those who, for reasons too well known and too desperate to need elaboration, constitute a kind of third world of the mind. As a Latin American, this accusing presence gives me a bad conscience which I share with many other writers and which cannot be salved by intellectual discussion among colleagues. At the same time I realize that it is not the writer's job to engage in political combat; poetry, fiction and experiments in writing are the essential reason for his work and the work of his reason. To attain a balance, a viability between both these things is a goal as arduous as it is desperate; thus it is not astonishing that, in the majority of cases, writers are divided into those who opt for political literature and those who confine themselves to pure creation. In Latin America, and I refer especially to the southern part, this choice collides with a reality which rejects it. It is true there are small minority groups of readers for either a militant or a pure literature. But there is an overwhelming majority of readers for whom literary reading has, at the same time, to satisfy a profound necessity for entertainment and an immediate preoccupa-

Something More than Words

tion, *hic et nunc*, for an authentic identity, a dignity and an individual and a collective liberty which is denied them by the enemies within and without.

Even if this general situation of the reader and the writer is pertinent to many countries in many parts of the world, I think that it is now reaching a critical point in the southern part of Latin America. Deliberately dispossessed of themselves as individuals as well as communities, the peoples of Argentina, Chile, Uruguay, Paraguay and Bolivia (not forgetting Brazil, muzzled now for so many years) find themselves in the situation of prisoners deprived not only of communication with the outside world but also with their fellow-captives. That is why, although this constitutes the centre of the problem which concerns millions of people on this planet including thousands of intellectuals living in their countries or exiled from them, I emphasize the situation of my own nation and put myself on the same level as many others as an exiled Latin American who cannot and does not want to continue working as a writer on the margin of this daily hell. For more than twenty years I have lived in Europe of my own free will because doing so implied an individual fulfilment without cutting off the roots of my own nationality. The fact of feeling myself today a compulsory exile does not change my attitude and my work at all. As so many Latin Americans who wrote and write in Spanish thousands of miles away from their countries, I maintain contact with my imprisoned and reviled brothers, I write for them because I write in their language, which will always be mine. Together with many others I am looking for a way of helping them and bringing their liberation nearer . . . readers will always remain much more important to me than writers.

One should not have illusions about the total number of readers in Latin America, with the sole and admirable exception of Cuba. It is insignificant in relation to the great masses of partial and total illiterates. Within that more than negative panorama there has become apparent in the last twenty years a vertiginous increase in the number of readers who closely follow the work of our authors. Among them the greatest number are those who in their reading are searching for something more than entertainment or oblivion. Their reading is always more critical and demanding and tries to bring literature closer to actual experience.

Of this I will give you a simple example, which unfortunately could be multiplied *ad infinitum*. Last year I published a book of short stories in Spain, which was to come out simultaneously in Argentina. The government of my country let the publisher know that the book would only be printed if I accepted the suppression of two stories considered hostile to the regime. One of them told, without any political allusions, about a man who disappears suddenly in Buenos Aires; this story was hostile towards the military junta because in Argentina people do disappear daily and there is no way of getting any news about them. Disappearance has profitably replaced murder in the middle of the street or the discovery of the corpses of uncountable victims; the governments of Chile and Argentina, and the 'commandos' who support them, have established a technique that on the one hand permits them to pretend ignorance about the destiny of those who have vanished and on the other prolongs in a most horrible way the vain hopes of their families and friends. This has been the destiny of an Argentine novelist called Haroldo Conti and the same has happened to another writer called Rodolfo Walsh. But to quote two well-known names is like letting two drops of water fall into a vessel filled to the brink with others—almost all unknown, the names of workers, political militants, trade unionists, to which one could add lawyers, doctors, psychiatrists, engineers, physicists. Cases like that of the Rector of the University of Bahia Blanca, and that of the French nuns, which were widely published in the columns of the European press, are also minor in comparison with a reality which may have been somewhat alleviated thanks to strong international pressure. But it is far from over and done with, because the conditions which permit these disappearances remain unchanged. It is sufficient to know that the chief of the Argentine military junta retired from the army to continue as a civilian at the head of the government until 1981; whether military or civilian, the victims are always the same, just as those responsible are and will remain the same.

The second banned story described a clandestine visit which I made to the community of Solentiname by the great central lake of Nicaragua. There is nothing in it that could directly offend the Argentine junta, but everything is offensive which tells the truth about what is happening in so many Latin American countries; and this story was furthermore sadly prophetic since a year after I wrote it the troops of the dictator Somoza razed and destroyed this marvellous small Christian community, led by one of the great Latin American poets, Ernesto Cardenal. I make no apology for quoting my own works; they are the very mirror of so much other censorship that muzzles writers and readers in our country. It is true that we writers always find a way of writing and even publishing but on the other side of the wall there are the readers who cannot read without taking risks; on the other side the people whose only source of information is the official one; on the other side there is a generation of children and adolescents who, as in the case of Chile, are 'educated' to become perfect fascists, automatic defenders of the big words that disguise reality: fatherland, national security, discipline. God. . . . There are those who are not intellectuals who are of importance to me today; the fishermen, the peasants of Solentiname, the Chilean children, the vanished and tortured in Argentina and Uruguay, all and everyone of the circles of hell which constitute the southern part of Latin America. And not as literary subjects, that goes without saying, but as the motivating force which can still make me write and not think of myself as completely useless.

Unfortunately we know how very relative is the efficacy of writers when faced with the brutality of power in any of its forms. That is why, although I have made these unavoidable references to the situation in the southern part of Latin America, it is not these that I want to stress, but to deepen the dialectic of the reader and the author as a prime function of our profession. The cultural or spiritual values of this relation are obvious; what is not always evident is the degree to which the writer and the reader dissociate them from the other values that determine man's position as an individual and as a member of a community or of a whole people. What is, and above all what ought to be, the impact of a creative work in this situation? The optimistic equating of culture with freedom and happiness fell to the ground some time ago together with other myths of humanism; but this has not freed us, as writers, from responsibility towards the reader.

Yesterday's reader waited for the books which came into his hands more or less by chance; today's reader in many direct and indirect ways demands them. A Latin American writer who achieves a certain recognition and is known to have democratic views is besieged by correspondence which to a large extent goes far beyond critical comments since it contains a desire and readiness for dialogue, which has nothing to do with the admiring passivity of other periods in the history of literature. The demands of the Latin American reader are above all personal, they form a request and a hope for responsibility from the author. In many cases, of course, they identify him with a political movement, but what is really important is something else, it is the terrible anxiety to draw closer to the literary work of one's choice in a manner which may bring the author closer to the reader on every level. Thus the writer has already taken the first step in the measure to which his work and/or his political position is sufficiently clear for the reader to know whom to write to and it is obvious for example that an Argentine reader, conscious of what the regime of the military junta implies, is not going to waste the price of stamps in writing to Jorge Luis Borges. But this first step, this first definition of the writer, is never enough for the majority of our readers; their letters, their questions contain much more than an affirmation of nearness in a domain much wider than literature. This quest ties the reader to the writer in the field not only of culture but of destiny, of mutual progress towards the fulfilment of liberty and identity. It is easy to imagine that this search of the reader for contact with the writers of his continent multiplies the unease and the wrath of all the dictators; when the Chilean junta burned thousands of books in the streets of Santiago, they were burning much more than paper, much more than poems and novels; in a sinister way they burned the writers of these books and those for whom they had been written.

In Mexico, in Venezuela, in Costa Rica I have given lectures about literature to a vast public, consisting mainly of university students and young writers. At question time each one approaches me as a reader, but as an eager and anxious reader, a reader for whom literature is part of life and not of leisure, a part of politics and history. I never felt more strongly the difference between this type of Latin American reader and that of other cultures where literature still keeps a primordially entertaining function; amongst us, writing and reading becomes more and more a possibility of acting outside the bounds of literature, although the majority of our more significant books do not contain explicit messages. In the work of writers like Neruda, Asturias, Carpentier, Arguedas, Cardenal, García Márquez, Vargas Llosa and many others, the reader finds more than just poems, more than novels and tales, without these books necessarily containing explicit messages. He finds signs, indications, questions rather than answers, but questions that put a finger on the most naked of our realities and weaknesses; he finds traces of the identity we are searching for, he finds water to drink and the shade of trees in the dry roads and in the implacable spaces of our alienated lands. But he also finds in them the brotherhood and contact which the reader demands and which these authors that I have mentioned, and many more, give him without shunning any of their responsibilities as writers and as individuals.

The writer does not lack opportunities to accept this global attitude—perhaps unfortunately, since it is always a question of facing disgrace, violence and even genocide both physical and cultural. Just recently there were reports in the press that the ambassador of the United States had delivered to the Argentine junta a list of the political prisoners compiled by their information services, containing a total of ten thousand names. Irony, which is one of the most fruitful attributes of literature, finds here a choice ground; is it not ironical that this enormous list should be in proportion to a country whose imperialist credo and whose arts of appropriation and of oppression in Latin America are too well known. It is ironical that a system capable of contributing decisively to the fall of the democratic regime of the *Unidad Popular* in Chile now tries to solve the murder of Orlando Letelier, and that after having openly favoured so many military dictatorships in Argentina, it is now indignant about the number of political prisoners in the country.

Oblivion is perhaps a sanity-saving necessity in man but also an ignoble distortion of truth; that is why I would like to thrust in front of the forgetful the documents of the second Bertrand Russell Tribunal, which for many years collected overwhelming evidence about US intervention in the countries of Latin America. I do it, moreover, to show that the writer in many cases is able to respond with actual deeds to those demands of his readers which I have spoken of before. During the work of the Russell Tribunal three intellectuals were present as members of the jury whose literary work has nothing to do with the proselytism or political message so often demanded of authors; I refer to Armando Uribe, a Chilean poet and diplomat, to Gabriel García Márquez, and to myself. I think that for many of our readers this long work of denunciation and testimony will have confirmed what they expect from a writer beyond his books. Anyhow, I know that I can go on writing my purely literary fiction without being accused by those who read me of being an escapist; so this does not give me a bad conscience. What we writers can do is insignificant in the face of the panorama of horror and oppression that the southern part of Latin America presents today; nevertheless we must do it and indefatigably seek new ways of intellectual struggle.

Witness in Difficult Times
RODOLFO WALSH

Rodolfo Walsh was a well-known investigative journalist in Buenos Aires. In March 1977 he sent an 'Open Letter' to the Argentinian military junta and 'disappeared' the following day— one of the thousands of Argentinian desaparecidos *whose fate has never been established. Rodolfo Walsh's 'Open Letter' appeared in* Index on Censorship *later that year.*

Press censorship, the persecution of intellectuals, a recent police raid on my house, the murder of dear friends, and the loss of a daughter who died fighting the dictatorship, are some of the circumstances which oblige me to adopt this form of clandestine expression after having worked openly as a writer and a journalist during almost thirty years.

The first anniversary of the present military junta has been the occasion for many official documents and speeches evaluating the government's activities during the past year. However, what you call successes were, in fact, failures; the failures that you have recognized were crimes; and you leave out all mention of the calamities.

On 24 March 1976 you overthrew a government in which you had all participated. Illegitimate in its origin, your government could have established its legitimacy by returning to the kind of programme which had the support of 80 per cent of the electorate in 1973. That programme remains the valid expression of the will of the people, which is the only possible interpretation of the 'national spirit', to which you appeal so often.

By rejecting that road, you have restored a totally bankrupt current of ideas representing the interests of an obsolete minority. This tiny minority blocks the development of our productive potential, exploits our people, and dismembers our country. Such a policy can be pursued, in the short term, by prohibiting political activity, taking over the trade unions, gagging the press, and spreading the most savage reign of terror Argentina has ever known.

Fifteen thousand people missing without trace (*desaparecidos*), 10,000 prisoners, 4000 dead, and tens of thousands of exiles are the statistical bones of this terror.

Having filled the existing prisons, you created virtual concentration camps in all the principal military bases, where no judge, lawyer, journalist or international observer may enter. The military secrecy of the proceedings, which you claim to be essential to your investigations, means that most arrests are in fact kidnappings, which allow torture without limit and executions without trial.

In this way you allow torture to continue indefinitely. The arrested person does not exist. There is no possibility of the prisoner being brought before a judge within ten days as the law requires, a law which was previously respected even during the darkest days of former dictatorships.

There is no limit on the time, neither is there any restriction on the methods used. These are a throwback to the Middle Ages, when torturers amputated the limbs of their victims or eviscerated them. Now it is done with surgical and chemical instruments which medieval executioners did not have at their disposal. The rack, thumbscrew, flaying, and saws of the Inquisition reappear in prisoners' testimony, along with the electric prod, the 'submarine' and the air-compressor of contemporary torture.

The premise that the extermination of the guerrilla justifies all methods of repression has led you further and further into the metaphysical realm, in which the original objective of extracting information through the use of torture is subordinated in the perverted minds of those who administer the torture to the need to utterly destroy their victims, depriving them of all human dignity, which both the torturers and yourselves have already lost.

The refusal of the junta to publish lists of prisoners covers up the systematic slaughter of prisoners, which goes on in the early hours of the morning, under the pretence of gun-battles with guerrillas or attempts to escape.

These victims of reprisal are used as hostages by the authorities. Many of them are trade unionists, intellectuals, relatives of known guerrillas, unarmed political dissidents, or simply suspicious in the eyes of those who detained them. They are the victims of a doctrine of collective guilt, which long ago disappeared from the norms of justice in any civilized community. They are utterly incapable of influencing the political developments which give rise to the events for which they are murdered. They are killed to balance the number of dead on either side, in accordance with the body-count principle first employed by the Nazi Germans in occupied countries in Europe, and afterwards refined by the American invaders in Vietnam.

The summary execution of guerrillas who are injured or captured in real combats is also clear from the official military communiqués, which last year claimed 600 dead and only fifteen wounded among the guerrillas, a percentage which is unheard of in even the most savage conflicts.

More than 100 prisoners, who had already been brought before the courts, have been killed in alleged escape attempts. The official version is again designed not so much to be believed as to warn the guerrilla and the political parties that the recognized political prisoners are a strategic reserve for reprisals, at the disposal of the army commanders, depending on their mood, the course of the war, or administrative convenience.

The murder of Dardo Cabo, arrested in April 1975 and shot down in prison on 6 January 1977, together with seven other prisoners in the power of the First Army Corps, commanded by General Carlos Suarez Masón, revealed that these episodes are not the exceptional acts of a few mad 'centurions'. You plan them at the highest level, discuss them in cabinet meetings, order them as commanders of the three services, and approve them as members of the ruling junta.

Between 1500 and 3000 people have been killed in secret since you prohibited any information concerning the discovery of corpses, which have in some cases been impossible to hide because of the numbers of victims involved or because the deaths affect other countries.

A skin-diver found a virtual mortuary on the bottom of the San Roque lake near Cordoba. He reported his macabre discovery to the police, but his testimony was not accepted. He wrote to the newspapers, but nothing was ever published.*

The pattern of killing removes any remaining credibility from the fiction of autonomous right-wing death squads, supposed heirs of the Triple-A of José López Rega. To accept their existence, one has to believe them capable of entering the largest military base in the country (Campo de Mayo) in army trucks, carpeting the River Plate with bodies, and throwing prisoners into the sea from the planes of the First Airborne Brigade, without General Videla, Admiral Massera or Brigadier Agosti (the three commanders of the armed forces and members of the junta) knowing anything about it. The Three As today are the three arms of the military, and the junta, which you constitute, is not the point of balance between 'opposed violences', nor is it the just judge standing between 'two kinds of terrorism', it is rather the very source of the Terror, which is now running out of control with death its only message.

*Letter from Isaías Zanotti, published by ANCLA (clandestine news agency).

The certain participation in these crimes of the Department of Foreign Affairs of the Federal Police, directed by officers trained by the CIA through AID, such as Police Commissioners Juan Gattei and Antonio Getter, who themselves take orders from Mr Gardener Hathaway, station chief of the CIA in Argentina, is the seedbed of future revelations similar to those which today shock the international community. These revelations will not be exhausted even when they expose the role of the CIA, along with senior officers of the army, headed by General Benjamín Menéndez, in the creation of the Libertadores de America Lodge, which replaced the Triple-A until its global functions were assumed by the junta in the name of the three services.

This dramatic picture of extermination also includes the prosecution of entirely personal vendettas, as in the murder of Captain Horacio Gandara, who for more than ten years had been investigating the shady business deals of senior naval officers, or the murder of Horacio Novillo, a journalist employed by *Prensa Libre*, which published details of the links between Economy Minister José Martínez de Hoz and multinational businesses.

In the light of such incidents we begin to understand the full significance of the definition of the war being waged by the armed forces, according to one senior officer: 'The struggle we are engaged in does not recognize any natural or moral limits; it is beyond any discussion of what is good or evil'.

These events, which have already shaken the conscience of the civilized world, are not the greatest sufferings undergone by the Argentine people, nor the worst violations of human rights for which you are responsible. In the economic policies of the government, one finds not only the explanation for its repressive crimes, but also a greater atrocity which punishes millions of human beings with carefully planned misery. . . .

These are the thoughts which I wished to share with the members of the junta on this first anniversary of your disreputable government, without hope of being listened to, in the certainty of persecution, but faithful to the commitment I made a long time ago to bear witness in difficult times.

Translated by Christopher Roper

Last Will and Testament
ARIEL DORFMAN

Ariel Dorfman is a Chilean writer who in 1983 was permitted to return to his country after ten years of exile in Europe and the USA. 'Last Will and Testament' is one of a series of poems he dedicated to the 2500 of his fellow countrymen estimated to have 'gone missing' since General Pinochet's coup of September 1973. The poem appeared in Index on Censorship *in 1979.*

Last Will and Testament

When they tell you
I'm not a prisoner
don't believe them.
They'll have to admit it
some day.
When they tell you
they released me
don't believe them.
They'll have to admit
it's a lie
some day.
When they tell you
I betrayed the party
don't believe them.
They'll have to admit
I was loyal
some day.
When they tell you
I'm in France
don't believe them.
Don't believe them when they show you
my false I.D.
don't believe them.

Last Will and Testament

Don't believe them when they show you
the photo of my body,
don't believe them.
Don't believe them when they tell you
the moon is the moon,
if they tell you the moon is the moon,
that this is my voice on tape,
that this is my signature on a confession,
if they say a tree is a tree
don't believe them,
don't believe
anything they tell you
anything they swear to
anything they show you,
don't believe them.

And finally
when
that day
comes
when they ask you
to identify the body
and you see me
and a voice says
we killed him
the poor bastard died
he's dead,
when they tell you
that I am
completely absolutely definitely
dead
don't believe them,
don't believe them,
don't believe them.

Translated by Edie Grossman

In Defence of the Word
EDUARDO GALEANO

Eduardo Galeano, a leading Uruguayan writer and journalist, was Editor of the weekly Marcha *(1961–4) and later founded the magazine* Crisis *in Buenos Aires. He now lives in Spain. 'In Defence of the Word' came out in* Index on Censorship *in 1977.*

During long sleepless nights and days of depression, a fly buzzes and buzzes around the head: 'Writing, is it worth it?'

In the midst of the farewells and the crimes, will words survive?

Does this profession, which one has chosen or which has been chosen for one, make any sense?

I am South American. In Montevideo, where I was born, I edited some newspapers and journals; one after the other they were closed down, by the government or by the creditors. I wrote several books: they are all banned. At the beginning of '73, my exile began. In Buenos Aires, we founded *Crisis*. It was a cultural journal with the biggest circulation in the history of the Spanish language. In August of last year its last number appeared. It could not continue. When words can be no worthier than silence, it is better to say nothing. And to hope.

Where are the writers and journalists who produced the journal? Almost all have left Argentina. Some are dead. Others, imprisoned or disappeared.

In such stormy times, the profession of writing is dangerous. In such circumstances, one recovers pride and joy in words, or loses respect for them for ever.

1. One writes out of a need for communication and communion with others, to denounce pain and share joy.

In Defence of the Word

One writes against one's own solitude and that of others. One assumes that literature transmits knowledge and acts upon the language and conduct of those who receive it, that it helps us to know ourselves better so as to achieve a collective salvation. But 'others' is too vague a term, and in time of crisis and of definition, the ambiguity can come too close to a lie. One writes in fact for the people whose situation one feels identified with, the undernourished, those who cannot sleep, the rebels and the oppressed of this world; and the majority of them cannot read. And of the minority who can, how many can afford to buy books? Is this contradiction resolved by proclaiming that one writes for that convenient abstraction called 'the masses'?

2. We have the fortune and misfortune to belong to a tormented part of the globe, Latin America, and to be living during a historical period which hits us hard.

For those of us who want to work for a literature which will help to manifest the voice of those who have no voice, the question becomes, how can we act within this reality? Can we make ourselves heard in a deaf and dumb culture? Our countries are republics of silence. Is not the small freedom of the writer sometimes the proof of his failure? How far can we reach and who can we reach?

It is an admirable task to proclaim the world of the just and the free and a worthy role to deny the system of hunger and cages—visible or invisible. But how far away is the frontier? How far do the owners of power give permission?

3. Much has been said about the forms of direct censorship used by various regimes, such as the prohibition of inconvenient or dangerous books or periodicals and the destiny of exile, prison or death dealt out to some writers and journalists.

But indirect censorship operates more subtly. That it is less obvious does not make it less real. Little is said about it. Nevertheless it is what defines most profoundly the oppressive and prohibitory nature of the system from which the majority of our countries suffer. What does it consist in, this censorship which dares not tell its name? It means that the ship doesn't sail because there's no water in the sea: if 5 per cent of the population of Latin America can buy refrigerators, what percentage can buy books? And what percentage can read them, feel the need for them, receive their influence?

Latin American writers, in the pay of a cultural industry which serves the consumption of an educated elite, belong to a minority which they also write for. This is the objective situation of writers whose work confirms social inequality and the ruling ideology; it is also that of those of us who seek to break with these things. We are blocked by the rules of the reality within which we act.

The present social order perverts or destroys the creative capacity of the vast majority of men and limits the possibility of creation—ancient response to human pain and the certainty of death—to the professional efforts of a handful of specialists. How many of these 'specialists' are there in Latin America? Who do we write for, who do we reach? What is our real public?

Let us be wary of applause. Sometimes congratulation comes from those who think us harmless.

4. One writes to put death off the scent and to strangle the ghosts that pursue one within; but what one writes can be historically useful only when it coincides in some way with a collective need for the conquest of identity. What one would like to happen is I think this, that in saying 'This is what I am' and offering himself, the writer could help many other people to become conscious of what they are. As a means of revealing collective identity, art should be

considered a prime necessity and not a luxury. But in Latin America access to the products of art and culture is forbidden to the vast majority.

For people whose identity has been destroyed by successive conquering cultures, and whose ruthless exploitation is part of the machinery of world capitalism, the system creates a 'mass culture'. Culture *for* the masses would be a more adequate definition of this degraded art with a massive circulation, which manipulates consciousness, masks reality and tramples on the creative imagination. Useless for revealing identity, it is a way to wipe it out and deform it, to impose ways of life and patterns of consumption which receive massive diffusion through the media. What is called 'National culture', is the culture of the ruling class, which lives an imported life and limits itself to copying, abortively and in bad taste, so-called 'world culture', or what that is understood to be by those who confuse it with the culture of the dominant countries. In our period, the era of multiple markets and multinational corporations, internationalism applies not just to economics but to culture, 'mass culture', thanks to the accelerated development and massive diffusion of the media. The centres of power export to us not just machines and patents but also ideology. If in Latin America the enjoyment of the good things of the earth is reserved for the few, the majority has to be resigned to consuming fantasies. Illusions of riches are sold to the poor, and of freedom to the oppressed, dreams of triumph for the defeated and of power for the weak. There is no need to be able to read in order to consume the symbolic justifications for the unequal organization of the world disseminated by television, radio and the cinema.

To ensure the perpetuation of the current state of affairs in lands where every minute a child dies of disease or hunger, we have to be taught to see ourselves through the eyes of the oppressor. People are trained to accept 'this' order as the 'natural' order and therefore as an eternal one; and they identify the system with patriotism, so that an opponent of the regime is a traitor or a foreign agent. The law of the jungle, which is the law of the system, is sanctified, so that defeated peoples should accept their situation as their destiny. The falsification of the past pushes out of sight the true causes of the historical failure of Latin America, where poverty has always fed the prosperity of others: on the small screen or on the big one, the best man wins, and the best is the strongest. Wastefulness, exhibitionism and lack of scruple produce not disgust but admiration; everything can be bought, sold, rented, consumed—not excluding the soul. Magical properties are given to a cigarette, a car, a bottle of whisky or a watch: they provide personality, make you succeed in life, give you happiness. The proliferation of foreign models and heroes goes with the fetishism surrounding products and fashions from the rich countries. Our home-produced photo-romances and TV serials take place in a limbo of cheap illusion, on the margin of the real social and political problems of each country, and the serials we import sell western Christian democracy together with violence and tomato sauce.

5. In these lands full of youth, where young people incessantly multiply and cannot find employment, the ticking of the time bomb forces those in power to sleep with one eye open. Multiple methods of cultural alienation, machines for doping and castrating become more important every day. Methods for sterilizing consciousness are carried out more successfully than plans for birth control.

The best way to colonize a consciousness is to eradicate it. Operating to this end, whether consciously or not, is the importation of a false counter-culture which is finding increasing adherents among the younger generations in Latin American countries. Those countries which, because of their ossified structures or asphyxiating mechanisms of repression, exclude youth from political participation offer the most fertile ground for the proliferation of a supposed 'protest culture', which comes from outside as a by-product of the society of idleness and waste.

The habits and symbols of the rebellion of youth in the sixties in the USA and Europe came from a reaction against the uniformity of consumerism, but now they are themselves the objects of mass production. Clothes with psychedelic designs are sold in the name of 'liberation'; music, posters, haircuts and dresses which reproduce the aesthetic models of drug hallucination are part of a large-scale industry which throws them at the Third World. Together with the attractive coloured symbols, youth who want to escape from hell are offered tickets to limbo. The new generations are invited to abandon the pain of history for nirvana. Certain sections of Latin American youth, when they incorporate themselves into this drug culture, achieve the illusion of reproducing the way of life of their metropolitan counterparts.

This false counter-culture has nothing to do with our real needs for identity and destiny: it offers adventures for paralytics; it generates resignation, egoism, non-communication; it leaves reality intact but changes its image; it promises love without pain and peace without war. Furthermore, in turning sensations into articles for consumption, it fits perfectly into the 'supermarket ideology' which the mass media disseminate. If the fetishism of cars and refrigerators is insufficient to eliminate anguish and pacify anxiety, you can buy peace, excitement and happiness in the clandestine supermarket.

6. To arouse consciousness and reveal the true reality: can literature lay claim to a better role in these times and in these countries of ours? The culture of the system, culture of surrogates for life, masks reality and anaesthetizes

consciousness. But what can a writer do, however much his own fire burns, against the ideological machinery of lies and conformism?

If society tends to organize itself in such a way that no one ever meets anyone else, and reduces human relations to the sinister operation of competition and consumption—lone men using each other and smashing up against each other—what can be achieved by a literature rooted in fraternal bonds and participatory solidarity?

We have reached a point where to name things is to denounce them: Before whom? For whom?

7. Our destiny as Latin American writers is bound up with the necessity for profound social change. To tell is to give oneself: it seems obvious that literature, as the striving for full communication, will continue to be thwarted at the outset so long as there is misery and illiteracy and those in power carry on with impunity, fostering collective imbecility through the mass media.

I do not share the view of those who claim for the writer a privileged freedom unconnected with the freedom of other workers. Major changes of structure must occur in our countries for writers to reach beyond the closed citadels of the elites and express themselves without being gagged, visibly or invisibly. Within an imprisoned society, literature can only exist as denunciation or hope.

In the same sense, I believe it would be a dream to suppose that there is an exclusively cultural way of liberating the creative capacity of people when it has been kept oblivious by harsh material conditions and the struggle for survival.

8. Furthermore, can a national culture really be achieved in countries where the material foundations of power are not national, or depend on foreign centres?

If independence is not possible, what meaning is there in writing?

There is no 'degree zero' of culture, just as there is none in history. If we recognize an inevitable continuity between the stage of domination and the stage of liberation in any process of social development, why deny the importance of literature and its possible revolutionary function in exploring, revealing and disseminating our true identity or its projection? The oppressor wants the mirror to give to the oppressed no more than its blank silver. What process of change can urge forward a people which doesn't know who it is nor where it comes from? If it doesn't know who it is, how can it know what it deserves to be? Cannot literature directly or indirectly aid this revelation?

I believe the possibility of such a contribution depends to a great extent on the intensity of the writer's communion with the roots, the vicissitudes and the destiny of his people. And on the capacity of his sensibility to perceive the pulse and rhythms of the authentic counter-culture as it comes into being. Often what is considered as 'lack of culture' contains the seeds of fruit of the 'other' culture, the one which opposes the dominant culture and shares neither its values nor its rhetoric. It is often mistakenly despised for being a mere degraded repetition of the 'cultured' products of the elite or of cultural models mass-produced by the system, but often a popular narrative can be more revealing and valuable than a 'professional' novel, and the pulse of real life is felt more strongly in certain anonymous songs that belong to local tradition than in many books of poetry written in the code of the initiated. The testimony of people expressing their sufferings and hopes in a multiplicity of ways is often more eloquent and beautiful than works written 'in the name of the people'.

Our genuine collective identity comes from the past and is nourished by it—footprints which our own feet follow, steps which foreshadow our paths in the present—but does not crystallize into nostalgia. Certainly, we are not going to find our hidden face in the artificial perpetuation of ethnic dress, customs and objects which tourists demand from conquered nations. *We are what we do, and above all what we do to change what we are*: our identity lies in action and struggle. That is why the revelation of what we are implies denunciation of what prevents us being what we can be. We define ourselves through defiance and through opposing obstacles.

A literature born of crisis and change and deeply immersed in the risk and adventure of its time, can certainly help to create the symbols of the new reality and perhaps illuminate—if talent and courage are not lacking—the signs that show the way.

9. The number of copies published or the amount of sales do not always give a true measure of a book's effect. Sometimes a written work gains an influence which is much wider than its apparent diffusion; sometimes it provides answers years in advance to collective problems and necessities, if the artist has actually lived them as doubts and tensions inside himself. The work springs from the wounded consciousness of the writer and is projected into the world: the act of creation is an act of solidarity which does not always fulfil its destiny during the life of the person who accomplishes it.

10. I do not share the view of writers who ascribe to themselves divine privileges not granted to ordinary mortals, nor that of those who beat their breast and tear their clothing asking for public dispensation to live in the service of a useless vocation.

Neither gods nor insects. Consciousness of our limitations is not consciousness of impotence: literature, a form of action, has not supernatural powers, but the writer can achieve his measure of magic when he secures the survival, through his work, of people and experiences that have a real value.

If what he writes is not read with impunity but changes or stimulates the reader in some way, then the writer can lay claim to his part in the process of change: without pride or false humility and knowing himself to be part of something much vaster.

It seems logical to me that language is belittled by those who cultivate a monologue with their own shadows and endless labyrinths. But words have a meaning for those of us who want to celebrate and share the certainty that the human condition is not a sewer. We look for people to communicate with, not admirers, we offer dialogue, not spectacle. We write from a striving for true meeting, so that the reader may be in communion with words that come to us from him and return to him as inspiration and prophecy.

11. To claim that literature on its own will change reality would be an act of arrogance or madness. It seems to me no less stupid to deny that in some degree it can help to bring about change.

Consciousness of our limitations is fundamentally consciousness of our reality. In the fog of hopelessness and doubt it is possible to confront things face to face and fight them out body to body: starting out from our limitations but in opposition to them.

In this sense, it is as much a desertion to write 'revolutionary' literature for the convinced as it would be to write conservative literature dedicated to the ecstasy of contemplating one's own navel. There are people who cultivate an 'ultra-left' literature, apocalyptic in tone, directed at a small public which already agrees with what is being said: what is the risk taken by these writers, however revolutionary they may claim to be, if they write for the minority who think and feel like them and give them what they expect to find? In that case there is no possibility of failure; but there can be no success either. What is the use of writing if not to defy the blockade which the system places round the dissident message?

Our effectiveness depends on our capacity to be audacious and astute, clear and attractive. Let us hope we can create a language with more energy and beauty than that which conformist writers use to salute the twilight.

12. But it is not just a problem of language. There is also the question of media. The culture of resistance uses all the media at its disposal and does not allow itself the luxury of wasting any means or opportunity of expression. Time is short, the challenge crucial and the task enormous: for the Latin American writer committed to the cause of social change, the production of books forms part of a struggle on a multiple front. We do not subscribe to the sacralization of literature as a congealed institution of bourgeois culture. Documentaries and reports for mass circulation, scripts for radio, cinema and television, and the popular songs are not always 'minor' genres, belonging to a subordinate category, as is believed by some marquises of specialized literary discourse who look askance at them. The cracks that the journalism of rebellion in Latin America has opened in the alienating machinery of the mass media have often been the result of a creative effort and sacrifice in no way inferior in aesthetic accomplishment and effectiveness to good fiction.

13. I believe in my craft; I believe in my instrument. I can never understand how writers could write while cheerfully declaring that writing has no meaning in a world where people are dying of hunger. Nor can I ever understand those who turn words into a target for fury or an object of fetishism. Words are a weapon and can be used for good or evil: the responsibility for the crime never lies with the knife.

I believe that the primordial function of contemporary Latin American literature is to rescue words from that frequent and impure degradation which has served to prevent or betray communication. 'Freedom' is, in my country, the name of a prison for political prisoners and 'democracy' the name for various regimes of terror; 'love' defines the relation of a man with his car and 'revolution' is understood as what a new detergent can do in your kitchen; 'glory' is what a particular toilet soap achieves and 'happiness' the sensation you get from eating sausages. 'Peaceful country' means, in many places in Latin America, 'ordered cemetery', and where it says 'sane man' one may have to read 'impotent man'.

By writing it is possible to offer, despite persecution and censorship, the testimony of our time and our people—for now and for posterity. One may write in order to say, in a sense: 'This is where we are, this is where we were; we are like this, this is what we were like.' Slowly gaining strength and form, there is in Latin America a literature which does not set out to bury our own dead, but to perpetuate them; which refuses to clear up the ashes and tries on the contrary to light the fire. That literature continues and enriches a powerful tradition of fighting words. If, as I believe, hope is better than nostalgia, perhaps this nascent literature may be worthy of the beauty of the social forces which will sooner or later, cost what it may, radically change the course of our history. And perhaps it may help to preserve for the youth to come, as the poet put it, 'the true name of each thing'.

Translated by William Rowe

Index on Censorship

'After I was banned I stopped writing. . . . I couldn't see the purpose of writing again. . . . Then *Index* published excerpts of my autobiography and a few of my poems. It really ignited me to see my name in print again and there was a whole surge of creativity.'
Don Mattera, South Africa

'Your piece on my case was the fairest, most thoughtful and most comprehensive I have seen anywhere.'
Daniel Schorr, journalist, USA

'I am deeply moved by your attention to my open letter which you printed in your publication. This event had an indirect influence on my destiny.'
Jonas Jurasas, former Director of Kaunas State Theatre, Soviet Lithuania

'The influence of *Index on Censorship* goes much further than you can see here in London. I was surprised that the editor and publisher of a very important newspaper in the city of Bahia Blanca in Argentina, a right-wing newspaper, practically a fascist newspaper, was impressed and worried when *Index* published a short item saying that his newspaper, *La Nueva Provincia*, is anti-Semitic.'
Jacobo Timerman, formerly editor of La Opinion, *Argentina*

A subscription for one year (6 issues) at 1984 rates costs £13.00 (Britain), $25.00 (USA) or £14.00 (rest of the world). Orders can be sent to *Index on Censorship*, 39c Highbury Place, London N5 1QP, UK.or in the USA to the Fund For Free Expression, 36 West 44th Street, New York, NY 10036.